The Crusades
A Beginner's Guide

Andrew Jotischky

ONEWORLD

A Oneworld Paperback Original

Published in North America, Great Britain and Australia by
Oneworld Publications, 2015

ISBN 978-1-78074-593-0
eISBN 978-1-78074-502-2

Contents

List of maps and illustrations

Maps

Figures

Timeline

1

What were the Crusades?

Toward the end of the first decade of the twelfth century, a monk from northern France sat down to write an account of the First Crusade, which had captured Jerusalem from the Seljuq Turks in 1099. He was looking back over the events of ten years before, in which a force of perhaps 60,000 mostly French, Flemish, Normans, Germans and Italians, including fighting men and unarmed pilgrims, men and women, had travelled from western Europe across the Balkans and modern-day Turkey into Syria, and south to Jerusalem. Only a fraction of the original force survived the three-year odyssey, but the remnants, battered by the climate, the hazards of travel and shortages of food and fodder for their horses, seized the city of Jerusalem amid scenes of slaughter in July 1099. The monk, Robert of Rheims, struggled to find a similar phenomenon with which to compare the First Crusade. In the end, he decided that it was, simply, the most important event in human history since the birth of Jesus Christ.

There are very few historical phenomena that are as susceptible to re-invention as the Crusades. The term has been used and re-used so many times since its original coining that it has come to have a much wider application than originally intended. For much of the twentieth century, in the Western world, 'crusade' was used metaphorically in public discourse and invariably in contexts where some moral virtue was to be associated in the reader's mind with the act of crusading. One of the most famous is *Crusade in*

Europe, the title used by General Dwight D. Eisenhower for his account of the D-Day invasion in 1944. But 'crusade' has also been used to describe campaigns for the public good in non-military spheres: we have become used to reading in newspapers about crusades against crime, against drugs, even litter. The carelessness with which the word has been used indicates its loss of real meaning, and this loss of meaning itself shows the amnesia of modern Western society about its past. The Crusades were a feature of a long-dead society in which religious values governed political action: an age of faith and of barbarism. In the West, at least, the Crusades were an anachronism, and the word could thus be re-used for more relevant social contexts.

This view of the Crusades tends to see them as a series of events more or less contingent on Western European society. One reason why the Crusades are still important, however, is because the First Crusade of 1095–9 was not a single event but a process. After the capture of Jerusalem in 1099, a small group of crusaders stayed in the East and established new states along the Levant coast from the south-east corner of modern-day Turkey to the Sinai peninsula. These territories – the Crusader States – were western European lordships in which political and economic control lay mainly in the hands of the descendants of the crusaders and subsequent immigrants: the Franks.

The Crusader States lasted about two hundred years on the Asian mainland before the Franks were themselves displaced by military conquest in 1291. Crusading itself, however, continued to take place well into the sixteenth century. Even before the fall of the Crusader States, crusading had been extended into other geographical areas: not only to places where Muslims lived, such as Spain, but into the north-east of Europe where the concept of holy war was applied against the pagan Livonians, and even into the heartland of Western Christendom, to aid in the Church's struggle against heresy. In the fourteenth and fifteenth centuries, the rise of the Ottomans aroused fears of a Turkish invasion of Christendom, and crusading changed its focus to mobilize Europeans to meet this new threat. Crusades in the later Middle Ages were launched against a wide variety of targets: not only the Turks, but also political enemies of the papacy. The Spanish Armada of 1588 borrowed from the language developed centuries earlier for crusading. The concept of holy war for the purposes of converting the world to Christianity, which became one of the justifications for crusading in the Middle Ages, was also used to rationalize the conquest of the New World by Spain in the sixteenth century.

Everyone knows, or thinks they know, what is meant by the term 'crusade', but even professional historians find it difficult to agree on a definition. One reason for this is that, surprisingly perhaps, the word 'crusade' was not used by or even known to the original crusaders. Instead, they were usually known simply as 'pilgrims', and the Crusades themselves as 'the business of the cross'. The word 'crusader' first appears in the twelfth century to describe someone who had 'signed himself with the cross' – literally, adopted the sign of the cross on his clothing as a public sign of his vow to undertake the holy war – but did not become common until about a hundred years after the First Crusade. As a noun describing an event or phenomenon – the holy war – the term took even longer to emerge and was not in common use until the seventeenth century. The implications of this are worth dwelling on. For one thing, it could suggest that people at the time had no real need for a special word to characterize what they were doing. Moreover, it could mean that they did not regard what we think of as crusading as anything particularly special. Perhaps a crusade was simply a different kind of war, waged against a new enemy – the Muslims – or in a particular part of the world. But this does not seem wholly convincing, because, in fact, we know that people *did* see the First Crusade (1095–9) as something special.

One reason we know this is the large number of accounts written of the crusade either soon after 1099 or in the next twenty years. The first, an anonymous account known as *The Deeds of the*

Franks, may have been written within the first twelve months of the capture of Jerusalem. It circulated widely and was taken back to western Europe to be read and copied as an authoritative version of the events of the expedition. *The Deeds of the Franks* is especially valuable because it is an eyewitness account, probably written by a cleric who accompanied one of the crusading contingents. Most of the contemporary or near-contemporary accounts were not by eyewitnesses, however, but by monks or other clerical writers – the professional historians of the day – who had read the *Deeds* or heard reports of the action from returning crusaders. In total, over a dozen such accounts survive. This figure does not include contemporary writings in which the crusade is mentioned as part of a larger series of events, but only those that were written specifically about the crusade. This is important because it was relatively unusual for writers to devote an entire book to a single event in this way. Most history-writing was in the form of a long chronicle, sometimes centred on the history of a particular monastery and beginning with its foundation. In such histories, regional, national and international events were described, but they were not the main purpose of the writing. The contrast between the reporting of the crusade and of the Norman Conquest of England in 1066, of which only about six contemporary accounts survive, is striking. For one thing, it shows the universal interest in the crusade across the whole of Christendom. For another, the fact that writers continued to find the crusade important subject matter even years after the events they were describing shows that interest in the crusade had not diminished. In fact, writers read and commented on each others' versions. One monastic chronicler, Guibert of Nogent, the abbot of Nogent-sous-Coucy in northern France, said in the preface to his *Deeds of God through the Franks* that his reason for writing was that he had recently read another account by an eyewitness, Fulcher of Chartres, and did not think it fit for purpose. An account of an event such as the crusade, explained Guibert, deserved to be written in much better style and with a more considered approach to the question of what the crusade was and how it should be seen as an event in human history. For Guibert, what mattered was not so much reporting what had happened between 1095 and 1099, but the meaning of these events in a larger scheme of understanding – real history, in other words, as classical authors had written it. The events themselves explained how God worked through human agency to accomplish his purposes, and the deeds of individuals provided moral examples of worthy or unworthy conduct.

None of these contemporary historians of the crusade seems to have thought that the events they were describing were the start of a new phenomenon that would be a feature of medieval life for centuries to come. Just as, after 1918, people looked back on 'the war to end all wars', in the years immediately after 1099 contemporaries had little reason to suppose that the events of what we call 'the First Crusade' would ever be repeated. Even those historians who continued their accounts after 1099, so as to cover the first generation of Frankish settlers in the East, did not write about the local wars in which they became embroiled in the course of establishing new states in the same way as they did the events of 1095–9. Doubtless because later crusades were unable to repeat the same military success, the conquest of Jerusalem in 1099 became a rallying cry for subsequent generations looking back to past glories. The knights who had stormed the walls of the city were lauded as Christian heroes, and the first Frankish ruler of Jerusalem, the crusader Godfrey of Bouillon, assumed legendary status in later medieval literature. Noble families invented crusading pedigrees in order to associate themselves in retrospect with the valorous crusaders of 1099. In launching a new crusade in 1145, Pope Eugenius III referred explicitly to the opportunity for a new generation of knights to cover themselves in glory as their grandfathers had done.

Surprisingly, given the impact that it had on contemporary and later writers, nobody could quite agree on how the crusade had

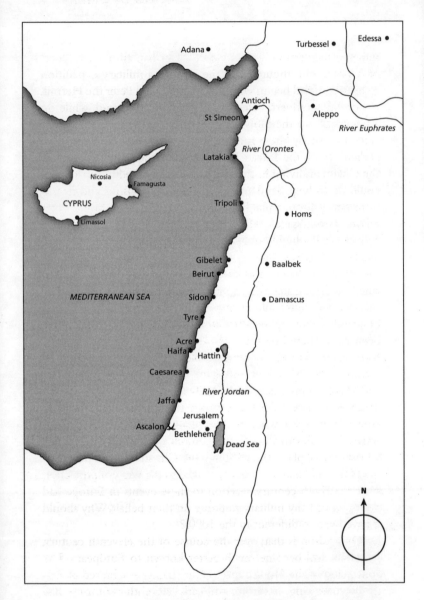

Map 1: The Crusader States

started. One version is recorded by a German chronicler, Albert of Aachen, who thought that the idea for a military expedition to Jerusalem had begun with a character called Peter the Hermit. According to Albert, Peter had been shocked to find, while on a pilgrimage to the Holy Land, how badly the local Christians were treated by their rulers, the Seljuq Turks. He sought an audience with the Patriarch of Jerusalem, the spiritual leader of the Christians living in the Holy Land, and asked what the West could do to help. Send an army to defeat the Turks and free us from persecution, replied the patriarch. Once back home, Peter relayed this message to the pope, who launched his crusade. The Seljuqs were a highly militarized people from central Asia who had taken over key positions of power in most of the Near East in the middle of the eleventh century. The Abbasid regime that had ruled the region since the eighth century had been weakened by succession disputes, and by about 1000 CE Egypt was in control of a rival Shi'ite regime, the Fatimids, while northern Syria had been reconquered by the Byzantine Empire. The Seljuqs, who had converted to Islam only a couple of generations before their arrival in the Near East, made life difficult for both Christian and Jewish communities in the Holy Land. There had been bouts of hostility toward Christians under the Abbasids and Fatimids, especially in 1009, when the Egyptian Fatimid ruler Al-Hakim ordered the destruction of the Church of the Holy Sepulchre, Christ's burial place. But although the Christian communities of the Holy Land had periodically looked to the West for protection since the ninth century, reaction to these events in Europe had not provoked any military response on their behalf. Why should it have been so different in the 1090s?

One reason is that, over the course of the eleventh century, Jerusalem had become much better known to Europeans. The conversion of the Hungarians to Christianity – achieved bloodily by their king, István, in the early eleventh century – had succeeded in opening up a previously unusable land route from

THE FRANKS

The term *francus* – more commonly its plural form, *franci* – came into prominence during the Crusades as a collective noun to describe the crusaders. Technically, Franks were the French-speaking inhabitants of the territories that came to make up France, but contemporary chroniclers needed a term to designate the collectivity of Westerners who embarked on crusades and settled in the East, to distinguish them both from the Muslim enemy and from the native inhabitants of the lands they conquered. Thus, in the terminology of crusading and the Crusader States, 'Franks' can mean not only French speakers but Germans, Italians and even English.

western Europe to Constantinople and the East. This meant that pilgrimage from the West, though still an uncertain and expensive undertaking, was within the bounds of possibility for more people. Consequently, large groups of pilgrims made the journey eastward to venerate the tomb of Christ. We have contemporary accounts of such massed pilgrimages from France and Germany in the 1020s, 1030s and 1060s. We also know of many individual noblemen and women who made the pilgrimage – sometimes, like the count of Anjou, Fulk the Black, going as many as three times. Pilgrimage to Jerusalem was encouraged and promoted by monasteries, and abbots set an example: at least half a dozen Norman abbots are known to have made pilgrimages to the Holy Land between the 1070s and 1090s. But monks and laypeople from France, England, Germany, Spain and Italy also flocked to Jerusalem. Relics were brought back from the Holy Land, and new churches were founded and dedicated to the Holy Sepulchre. In monasteries all over Europe, Easter was celebrated with re-enactments of the resurrection that involved processions made around wooden copies of the Holy Sepulchre. One German bishop, Meinwerk of Paderborn, even sent monks to Jerusalem to take the measurements of the Holy Sepulchre so as to be sure that the new copy he wanted to make would be accurate. Jerusalem, symbolized by the tomb of Christ in the Church of the Holy Sepulchre, had entered the European consciousness as never before. There was thus every reason for Europeans to respond to an appeal from the Christians of the Holy Land for deliverance from oppression – assuming that the story told by Albert was true. Although the details of his account of Peter the Hermit may reflect later invention, the essence of the story of an appeal to Western powers is not in itself implausible.

For most chroniclers of the time, however, the initiative came not from the East but from the West. According to the author of *The Deeds of the Franks*, the crusade happened when it did simply because the time was right. The knighthood of Europe responded to a widespread feeling that, in the words of the chronicle, the time had come for Christians to take up their cross and follow Christ – literally, to Jerusalem. But most of the chroniclers who wrote their histories after some years, and who were more reflective about the meaning of the crusade, thought that it must have begun with a flourish. The particular moment they saw as the beginning of the crusade was a church council summoned by Pope Urban II in November 1095 at Clermont-Ferrand, in the Auvergne region of south-central France. Here, on the penultimate day of the council, 27 November, Urban preached a rousing sermon to the assembled crowds in a field outside the town. Urban's famous 'crusading sermon' thus marks the starting point of what became a movement lasting hundreds of years and affecting untold millions of people across Europe and the Near East. It is particularly frustrating, then, that no single authoritative version of his words survives – only the reports of the four writers who turned the speech into the set piece that launched crusading. Before these reports can be examined, we first need to understand why Urban chose such an occasion and how the journey to Clermont had begun.

Urban II became pope in 1088 at a low point in papal fortunes. During the previous thirty years, the papacy had been struggling to assert itself as an office with truly international authority. The first step in this process, in 1059, was the creation of the College of Cardinals to elect new popes. Until then, popes had been chosen from among the more powerful Roman noble families, with the result that they had often been unable to act independently of the influence of these political forces. A reforming clique within the Church emerged during the middle years of the eleventh century and tried to end the dependence of the papacy on the Roman nobility. This group, headed between 1073 and 1085 by Pope Gregory VII, came into conflict not only with local entrenched interests but also with the most powerful political figure in Western Europe, the Holy Roman Emperor. The emperors thought themselves the successors not only to Charlemagne, who had revived the title in 800, but also to the Roman emperors of antiquity. The imperial title had since the middle of the tenth century been in the hands of the German royal dynasty that had succeeded Charlemagne's grandson Lothar. The defining moment of an emperor's career was his coronation, which could only be carried out in Rome by the pope. This meant that emperors, no matter how powerful they might be militarily, needed the approval of the pope in order to make their title a reality. But in the 1040s, the German King Henry III realized that the stranglehold exercised over the papal office by Roman noble families jeopardized his own authority. If he was to be able to make his imperial title real, he needed a pope he could trust – and, preferably, control. He also needed a figure who would be respected by the whole of Christendom – otherwise his own imperial title would be devalued. In 1046, therefore, a German army deposed the pope, Gregory VI, and placed Henry's own nominee, Clement II, on the throne of St Peter. There followed two generations of popes who were largely reformers, and who introduced a series of measures designed to take control of the papal office away from the Roman nobility. Most important, after the creation of the College of Cardinals to elect new popes, was the attempt to end secular kings' control over the process by which new bishops took office. Although these reforms were in some ways the logical outcome of Henry III's intervention in 1046, by the 1070s they had gone beyond what his successors were prepared to countenance.

In 1075, Pope Gregory VII, who had been a stalwart of reform behind the scenes years before his election, clashed with the German King Henry IV. The quarrel was initially over the question of which of them had the right to appoint the new archbishop of Milan. Because Holy Roman emperors laid claim to authority over the whole of northern Italy, Milan was a strategic target of great importance to them. Moreover, it mattered who became archbishop because Italy had no king of its own and the political power in the northern cities lay largely with the bishops. Gregory wanted a reformer who followed the papal agenda to be appointed, but Henry had his own candidate: a man, like many of the German bishops, who had been trained in royal administration and who would owe everything to his advancement by the king-emperor.

What started as a clash over a political appointment became a struggle for the levers of power in Christendom. At first, the only hold that Gregory had over Henry was that Henry had not yet been crowned emperor, and as long as he could deny him the imperial coronation Henry so coveted, the pope hoped Henry would agree to his demands. In 1076, Henry declared Gregory deposed, to which Gregory responded by excommunicating Henry. In January 1077, the pope lifted the sentence of excommunication only after humiliating the man who would be emperor by forcing him to kneel barefoot in the snow in front of him at Canossa, in northern Italy. Gregory demanded what popes had never claimed so forcefully before: recognition that he was the supreme authority in Christendom, by virtue of being the successor of St Peter, to whom Christ had given the keys to heaven. Henry, in response, invaded Italy in 1080, and by 1084 Gregory had been driven from Rome into exile. He died a year later, and for the next nine years the papacy struggled to assemble an alliance of forces that would enable it to return and to reassert its moral authority.

The conflict with the emperor forced the papacy to confront the realities of political power. Rhetoric was one thing, but resisting invasion required military strength, and the papacy had, as Stalin was to put it centuries later, 'no divisions'. What Gregory had at his disposal instead was an armoury of theological and spiritual power. In fact, previous popes had become increasingly interested in the question of how and in what circumstances force might justifiably be used. Alexander II had already, in the 1060s, approved the use of arms in the name of the Church in Spain, where the Christian kings of the north were trying to expand their power at the expense of the Muslim states in the peninsula, and even in the Norman invasion of England in 1066. In the 1080s, however, it was a question of how to defend the papacy against a stronger military power rather than of encouraging Christian kings to take lands to which the pope agreed they had a just claim. This required the recruitment and mobilization of troops, who had first to be persuaded that the papal struggle was a just cause. Supporters who sent troops included Matilda of Tuscany, the widow of Duke Godfrey of Lower Lotharingia (in western Germany), and Raymond IV, count of Toulouse, as well as local nobles and towns in north and central Italy. But in the end, what defeated Henry IV was not a superior military power but the addition to this network of alliances of some disaffected German nobles who rebelled against their king. This process, begun by Gregory VII and continued by Urban II after 1088, marked an important change in the political balance of Christendom. The papacy was now justifying interference in the internal affairs of a Christian kingdom on the grounds of the defence of the Church. As Gregory expressed it, what was at stake was the Church's liberty.

In the spring of 1095, that liberty appeared to have been secured. Henry was in difficulties with his rebel barons and Pope Urban was, for the first time, able to enter Rome in 1094. He held a council in the spring of 1095 at Piacenza in northern Italy, one of the purposes of which was to ratchet up the pressure on Henry. Among the people summoned to testify against Henry was his ex-wife. But, according to one chronicler, the Council of Piacenza was also noteworthy for the participation of another group of people: envoys from the Byzantine Emperor. There was nothing particularly remarkable in this. Although there had been a diplomatic rupture in relations between the papacy and the Byzantine government in 1054, Urban II had done his best to mend fences since becoming pope in 1088. The Byzantines did not subscribe to quite the same view of papal authority in the Church as did the reforming popes, but they recognized the prestige of the office held by the successor of St Peter. The significance of the Byzantine imperial presence at Piacenza was that the Byzantines wanted to ask for military help, and that they chose this forum in which to do so. Naturally, it was a situation that Urban sought to turn into a public relations triumph.

The Byzantine Empire reached the peak of its power and authority in the late tenth and early eleventh centuries. Northern Syria, including the city of Antioch, had been reconquered from the Abbasid caliphate, and new inroads were made into the Balkans by the great Emperor Basil II, 'the Bulgar-slayer'. Visitors to imperial Constantinople were bowled over by the grandeur of the imperial palace, by the churches and their relics, by the education and culture of the aristocracy, and by the sheer size and wealth of the city. For Byzantines, this was a natural state of affairs: their empire was simply the continuation of the Roman Empire and heir to its prestige and authority. They even called themselves 'the

Romans'. But successive generations of incompetent emperors exposed the structural weaknesses of the Byzantine system. In 1071 the Seljuqs turned their attention to Asia Minor (Turkey), the powerhouse of the Empire, the source of the bulk of its tax revenues and military manpower. The province fell like a house of cards. Deprived of financial resources and soldiers, the imperial government turned increasingly to paid troops from outside the Empire: Bulgars, Arabs, Armenians, Normans from southern Italy, English refugees from the Norman Conquest, Scandinavians. In the early 1090s a group of Flemish knights had served under the emperor. But by 1095 the Seljuqs had established a regional capital at Nicaea in western Asia Minor – alarmingly close to the imperial capital. Alexios Komnenos (emperor from 1081 to 1118) had skilfully kept the enemies of the Empire at bay while building up imperial influence in Cyprus and Syria, but he had been unable to prevent the fall of Antioch in 1086. Exactly what he wanted from Urban II in 1095 is not certain, but it is a mark of how far papal prestige had risen in the past few years that he saw appealing for papal help as the most effective way of spreading word of his need to recruit more foreign troops.

Urban seems to have done little initially about the Byzantine appeal. Perhaps he passed it on to interested parties, but if so no evidence of this survives. Instead, in the summer of 1095, he undertook a tour of France. This was a stately occasion designed to reinforce not only papal prestige but also papal authority. Like any ruler who wanted to exercise power, the pope had to travel in order to make his authority felt. He had to see what was going on in the provinces and dioceses of Christendom, and above all he had to exercise authority by hearing appeals and administering justice. Leadership meant acting as the court of highest appeal, and this could most effectively be done in person, rather than trusting the vagaries of letters sent by emissaries and legates. The tour of France was, therefore, a message that the pope was ready to take on the leadership of Christendom. Urban held local councils, consecrated churches and sat in judgement in disputes between bishops and monasteries. As a Frenchman, and former prior of the powerful monastery of Cluny, he was especially well placed to extend papal influence personally in French-speaking territories. He also met some of the most important political figures in France. In the 1090s, this meant the regional counts and dukes, rather than the king himself: men like the counts of Anjou and Toulouse. Significantly, both of these might have attracted his attention for other reasons. Count Raymond IV of Toulouse had been a supporter of the papal struggle against the emperor and had also taken part in the war against the Arabs in Spain. Count Fulk of Anjou had been on pilgrimage to Jerusalem. It seems likely that Urban raised with such men an idea that may have been developing in his thoughts since the spring of 1095, if not before. But it was not until the end of November that he made the idea public, at a council held in the town of Clermont, in the Auvergne. It was here, on the final day of the council, in a field outside the town, that he first introduced the idea of an expedition to liberate Jerusalem to a wider audience. For this reason, Clermont has been seen ever since as the birthplace of crusading.

What happened at Clermont? Curiously, for such an apparently crucial event in the history of Europe, nobody really knows – because no official record of the council proceedings or of Urban's address has survived. Instead, we have four accounts written not only years after the event but in full knowledge of the success of the crusade. The four 'Clermont chroniclers' – Robert of Rheims, Fulcher of Chartres, Guibert of Nogent and Baldric of Bourgueil – were looking back for a definitive starting point to the expedition launched in 1095, and they settled on Clermont. In contrast, *The Deeds of the Franks*, the earliest contemporary account, scarcely mentioned the council at all and instead gave the impression that the crusaders were responding to some kind of spontaneously felt zeitgeist. As we have already seen, another chronicler, Albert of Aachen, chose to attribute the initiative for beginning the crusade to the Christians of the East. But the consensus has come to be that Clermont was the moment at which all the developments in the papal reform movement over the previous generation coincided with a heightened sense of piety among laypeople to produce a spark of flame, which in turn was fanned by the uncertain political situation in the eastern Mediterranean.

It is worthwhile, therefore, to summarize what the chroniclers represented Urban as saying at Clermont. Three main themes emerge. First is the need to liberate Christians in the East from the violence done to them by the Seljuqs. A high degree of exaggeration was employed by the chroniclers, who put into Urban's mouth impassioned words describing torture, humiliation and destruction of property and holy places. Doubtless the general picture was based on anecdotal evidence, since we know from Eastern Christian and Jewish sources that the Seljuqs could be arbitrary in their treatment both of local non-Muslims and of Western pilgrims. But the chroniclers made it appear as though such episodes of violence were a deliberate and sustained Seljuq policy, and also that this policy entailed the relentless march of the Turks westward to threaten not only Constantinople but, eventually, the whole of Christendom. It is not only the threat that is significant here, but also the assumption on the part of Urban that it was the duty of Western Christendom to 'liberate' their brothers and sisters in the East. This kind of language only made sense because popes had been using terms such as 'the liberty of the Church' for twenty years or more in the context of their struggles against the emperor. It was, in a sense, simply the application of the same principle over a broader geopolitical map. But it also made sense because this was not the first encounter between Christians and Muslims in the second half of the eleventh century. Since the 1060s, the small Christian kingdoms of northern Spain, principally Castile and Aragon, had been pushing southward into territory held by independent Arab 'taifas' – the successor states to the caliphate of Cordoba, which had collapsed in 1031. The Reconquista was, pure and simple, territorial and economic expansion on the part of a small but highly militarized aristocracy at the expense of a more urban and prosperous society to the south. But it came to be inflected with a particular piety when knightly pilgrims on their way to the shrine of St James at Compostela, in Galicia, were encouraged to see a connection between their devotion to the saint and fighting against Muslim Arabs. Popes, particularly Alexander II and Gregory VII, were quick to capitalize on the possibilities. Although in 1095 the Reconquista was still largely free of the overtones and language of holy war, it formed a precedent in that knights from across the Pyrenees were already being recruited to participate in particular campaigns. Urban II used the language of liberation in encouraging knights to help retake Tarragona, in the county of Barcelona, from the Arabs in 1089.

A second theme in the reporting of Urban's Clermont preaching was the Holy Land. Jerusalem, declared Urban in the words of Baldric of Bourgueil, was not only the centre of the world but a holy relic. The place where Jesus had lived, worked miracles, suffered crucifixion and risen from the dead ought to be, Urban said, part of Christendom. It had been unjustly taken from Christians and it was now the obligation of the Christian knighthood to take it back, just as it was the duty of any vassal to defend the lands of their lord. Was God not the lord of all men? He relied on his faithful on earth to protect his rightful territory. Here again, Urban caught the mood of Christendom. This kind of rhetoric had resonance because of the popularity of pilgrimage to Jerusalem. What was new was the link between pilgrimage to the holy places and military action to take them into Christian possession. In hindsight it might look as though this was an obvious consequence of increasingly intense devotion to Jerusalem. However, it required a new kind of thinking on the part of the papacy to bring it about. Gregory VII had already given a hint in this direction in 1077. After the heir to the county of Barcelona, Peter Raymundi, murdered his stepmother, Gregory assigned

PILGRIMAGE

A spectacular programme of church building launched by Emperor Constantine (306–37) transformed Jerusalem into a city of churches and monasteries, and created the idea of the Christian Holy Land. The Arab conquests of the seventh century made pilgrimage from the West more difficult, but by the 1030s pilgrims were once again travelling in large numbers to the Holy Land. Many pilgrims went in massed groups, and there was an apocalyptic flavour to some eleventh-century pilgrimages. After 1099, once Jerusalem was under Christian control, pilgrims flooded to the Holy Land, and they continued to travel there in large numbers throughout the Middle Ages. The focal point of all pilgrimages was the Holy Sepulchre, but pilgrims also venerated the shrines of the Nativity in Bethlehem, the place of Jesus' baptism at the Jordan, the tomb of the Blessed Virgin at the foot of the Mount of Olives, and the many sites associated with Jesus' miracles. Most pilgrims travelled by sea, often in dangerous conditions. The demands of the journey were part of the purpose of pilgrimage, which was to do penance for one's sins. Undertaking a pilgrimage, especially to the Holy Sepulchre, was a temporal atonement for sins committed and confessed to a priest.

him a penance peculiar to the political situation. A normal penance for such a public crime of violence might have entailed a humiliating pilgrimage that would have removed Peter Raymundi from public affairs for a long period, perhaps even demanded that he enter a monastery and so remove himself forever. Either eventuality would have proved disastrous for Barcelona, on the front line of the Reconquista. Gregory's solution was to require Peter Raymundi to remain in Barcelona and to put his sword at the service of the defence of his inheritance against the Arabs. In miniature, this was effectively what Urban II appealed to the knighthood of France to do in 1095. The difference was that whereas Gregory VII could reasonably point to the need for Barcelona to have an heir of fighting age on the spot, in 1095 the threat was not to the actual lands of Western knights, but to the notional and symbolic 'inheritance' of Jesus, the Holy Land.

It was a revolutionary step taken by Urban to link the practice of pilgrimage with the idea of the legitimate defence of territory. It worked not only because of the appeal of the Holy Land but also because of the acceptance on the part of knights who took the cross that they needed to do penance. As a knight, one could scarcely help committing sins of violence. These, even though they might be legitimated by having been committed in service to one's lord, were nevertheless sins that required absolution and temporal satisfaction. Absolution came from confessing one's sins to a priest, temporal satisfaction from undertaking the penance assigned by one's confessor. Common among these, for the knighthood, was pilgrimage to a saint's shrine – not a holiday or pleasant tour, but a journey undertaken without arms, abstaining from sex and good living, and in the full consciousness that, until the penance was completed, one was an outcast from God's family. For sins of violence, a long period of quiet reflection without the possibility of doing further violence was required. Urban II overturned this way of thinking in 1095. In virtually the only independent piece of testimony we have from Clermont, apart from the chroniclers' accounts, Urban says that the expedition he was launching would be regarded as a penitential pilgrimage. It was war, but it was also a penance. Knights who needed to accomplish penance for sins of violence could now do so by committing further violence – but against the Seljuqs, for the recovery of the holy city.

According to Robert of Rheims, Urban understood very well why this appeal was likely to succeed. French knightly society, he regretted, was endemically violent because there was frenetic competition for land and inadequate central political authority to control it. The knighthood regarded war as a necessary means of securing their rights, defending their inheritances and exploiting their lands economically. Urban foresaw, in Robert's account of his preaching, that the armed pilgrimage would also offer opportunities for knights to settle in the Holy Land on conquered territory, thus relieving the pressures that made for such problems at home. Nowhere are we more conscious of Robert's hindsight than in this piece of reportage. By the time he was writing, Robert could look at twenty years or so of precarious but successful settlement in the East by survivors of the great expedition and subsequent émigrés. At Clermont, this lay far in the future and could hardly have been predicted.

2
An anatomy of crusading

The first step in launching a crusade was to proclaim the message of holy war: to preach the cross. After announcing his expedition in the autumn of 1095, Pope Urban II spent several more months in France, trying to persuade members of the higher nobility to take the cross. Because he could not be everywhere, he also delegated the task to others. We know very little about this process, but it seems likely that some kind of briefing instructions were prepared by the curia, or papal officials, because, as we shall see, the crusaders who left for the East in 1096 seemed to share the same ideas of where they were headed and why.

In the medieval Church, the job of preaching belonged to bishops, who were responsible for all aspects of Christian education in their dioceses. Parish priests rarely preached. For certain occasions, however, bishops also commissioned special preachers. Urban began the practice of employing special preachers to mobilize potential crusaders, and it was continued by his successors throughout the twelfth and thirteenth centuries. Some crusade preachers became very well known and were celebrated as spiritual performers for their ability to play on an audience's sensibilities. Preachers like Fulk of Neuilly travelled widely throughout northern Europe, drawing huge audiences.

The preaching of the Fifth Crusade, beginning in 1213, coincided with a new movement of spiritual awakening in Europe through preaching repentance; a movement inspired by the new orders of friars founded by St Francis of Assisi in Italy and St Dominic in southern France. As the orders of friars grew and developed, they became natural crusade preachers because, unlike bishops and clergy, they were trained for the job of preaching and spiritual motivation.

As occasions of preaching became increasingly formalized, the content also became more formulaic. By the middle of the thirteenth century, preaching manuals were being compiled so that the star preachers, such as the Dominican Stephen of Bourbon, could share their techniques.

What might those who attended crusade sermons expect to hear? The fundamentals of the message probably did not change much over time. Preachers reminded their audiences of the sanctity of the Holy Land and especially of the holy places in Jerusalem, and of the importance of safeguarding, in particular, the Holy Sepulchre, Christ's burial place. Sometimes, for example in preaching the First and Third Crusades, the supposed brutality and sacrilege of the Turks was a theme. The knighthood might be shamed into taking the cross by drawing attention to the disgrace of having allowed the holy places to fall into infidel hands. Especially after the establishment of the Crusader States, the fate of the settlers in the East at the hands of the Turks could also be part of the message. Sometimes visual aids were used: after the conquest of Jerusalem by Saladin in 1187, the Christian settlers in the East apparently sent back to the West a picture of a Turkish mounted warrior whose horse was shown urinating on the Holy Sepulchre. The emotional responsiveness of the audience was the preacher's best ally. Audiences were assured that taking the cross was not only justified but a necessary act to assure their own salvation. Preaching the Second Crusade in 1146, Bernard, abbot of Clairvaux, couched his appeal in business terms: any knight who could spot a good bargain would surely take up the offer of salvation. Miracles associated with taking the cross also became a staple of crusade preaching. Even before going to the East, simply taking the cross was enough to assure protection for the aspiring crusader. On the other hand, preachers warned their public against taking the vow lightly, or treating the crusade as everybody else's business rather than their own.

Preaching the crusade was already a carefully orchestrated occasion by the time Bernard addressed the court of King Louis VII of France at Easter 1146. An eyewitness describes weeping, applause and plenty of emotional release. The Third Crusade, a response to the fall of Jerusalem to Saladin in 1187, gave further opportunities for soul-searching. On the instructions of the pope, the crusade was preached in every diocese in Christendom. Bishops and clergy preached the cross not only in the original 'heartlands' of crusading – France, western Germany and northern Italy – but also in Scandinavia, central Europe, Spain and the British Isles. A detailed and colourful contemporary account of the archbishop of Canterbury's preaching tour in south Wales survives. It is clear from this account, by the archdeacon of St David's, Gerald of Wales, that the occasion was as important as the content. On a preaching tour hundreds of people would pour from the countryside into the towns at which the preacher spoke. Preaching was often preceded and followed by solemn processions of clergy carrying relics of local saints and was sometimes part of the celebration of a Mass. The music and theatre of the liturgy was part of the overall effect that made preaching more than simply a haranguing by an individual. Gerald tells us that he had already agreed to be the first to take the cross when Archbishop Baldwin preached, to set an example to others. Once a few people had declared themselves, peer pressure ensured that many others did the same. Back in 1095, knights who had taken the cross were already sewing crosses on to their clothing to give concrete expression to their symbolic action, and the sight of those who had already made the commitment, proudly wearing their crosses as a kind of uniform, must have had a profound effect on others. Gerald also did some of the preaching himself. Reading between the lines of his account, it seems safe to conclude that the actual content of a crusade sermon was less important than the occasion as a whole. People expected to be moved because they knew, more or less, what to expect from preachers. That did not mean, however, that they might not be caught up in the emotion of the occasion.

Taking the cross was one thing, actually going on crusade quite another. The emotions of the occasion led many to make commitments that they were in fact unable to keep. This became very clear when, in the early thirteenth century, bishops were required to keep records and check that those who had taken crusade vows had fulfilled them. In many cases, where, for example, people had taken the cross but fallen ill or been unable to find the money to go on crusade, there was nothing much that could be done, and the Church had to accept that in this respect the crusade was the victim of its own success. One consequence of the effectiveness of preaching was that many crusaders were recruited who were little better than arrow fodder.

One reason why so many people took the cross, even when they must have known they were unsuitable for the task of crusading, was that simply taking the cross granted certain privileges. These developed only gradually, but by 1215 anyone who took the cross enjoyed financial benefits, such as being able to take out interest-free loans, and gained freedom from legal proceedings. As early as 1149, a disillusioned German observer thought that the failure of the Second Crusade was due partly to most of the crusaders having taken the cross simply to escape from their obligations at home. As the legal implications of taking the cross came to be clarified still further, this must have become ever more likely: taking the cross meant deferring payment of interest on existing loans, and in some cases loans could be cancelled altogether.

This does not mean that cross-takers were all cynical opportunists. Contemporary accounts of crusade preparations from the late eleventh to the middle of the thirteenth centuries capture vividly the emotional excitement of the days and weeks leading up to departure. In 1095–6 there was as yet no blueprint for how the practicalities of departure were to be organized, but the main difficulty must always have been money. Although nobody knew how long their expedition would take, the practice of pilgrimage to the Holy Land was well enough established to allow crusaders to estimate that they would have to provide for themselves for several months. This required taking enough money to be able to replenish supplies of dry goods, buy fresh food en route, and also provide fodder for the horses when pasture was not available. Crusading armies were quite conservative when it came to their diet, mostly expecting to continue to eat the same kinds of foods while on active service as they did at home. This meant finding impractical quantities of flour or biscuit, meat and wine or beer. William of Rubruck, a Franciscan missionary who travelled widely in the Mongol territories of central Asia in the 1250s, remarked that if crusaders had been willing to eat as sparingly and infrequently as Mongols did when on the march, they would have been able to conquer the whole world.

Each knight had to provide weapons, armour and equipment not only for himself but for an entourage of foot soldiers befitting his status – usually about seven or eight, but sometimes considerably more. Knights who ran out of money could not rely on credit and had to trust to luck or plunder. Jean de Joinville, the seneschal of the county of Champagne, ran out of money to maintain his entourage of nine knights while the crusader army was wintering in Cyprus in 1248–9, a longer diversion than he had expected, and if King Louis IX had not taken him on in his own household, he would have had to beg his passage home.

Even wealthy knights did not have access to ready cash in very large quantities. In an agrarian economy such as medieval Europe, wealth was tied up in land and mostly measured in the agricultural surpluses needed to feed large retinues in one place. In order to feed people on the move, these assets had to be liquidated. There were economies of scale, naturally. Joinville clubbed together with his neighbours and relatives to equip a ship full of crusaders in 1248. Families might raise money to send one member on crusade. The investment entailed complex arrangements for converting property into money. The most straightforward method was to sell land. But this might mean depriving one's heirs, and given that there was no guarantee one would return home safely, crusaders wanted to do all they could to safeguard their inheritance. Other arrangements included mortgaging property, perhaps in the expectation that one might return home having made some money from plunder. More complex kinds of arrangements are recorded in deeds drawn up by departing crusaders. These show not only the means that crusaders resorted to in order to liquidate assets but also with whom such arrangements were made. Thus, for example, a knight called Bernard Morel agreed to let the nuns of Marcigny collect half the rent of his land while he was on crusade, and keep the rest against his return, all for a cash advance. Almost anything owned or controlled by landowners could be exchanged for cash: not only farms, vineyards and property, but jurisdictional and commercial rights to properties such as mills and ovens while crusaders were away.

The likeliest sources of such cash advances were monasteries, which were often in a position to collect cash as gifts or bequests from the laity. Monasteries, especially well-endowed ones, were part of the fabric of the landowning landscape throughout Europe. This meant that, like any other landowner, they were often embroiled in long-running land disputes with neighbouring families, possibly going back for generations. In order to take advantage of the potential that monasteries offered as lenders, knights who wanted to go on crusade had to settle such disputes. Consequently, one feature of the Crusades is the largely unintended function they performed of arbitrating in local political problems. For example, in 1197, before leaving for the East, Henry I of Brabant and Lorraine drew up a charter in which he abandoned all the claims he had previously made to woodland that was also claimed by the nuns of St Mary of the Forest. And fifty years previously, the northern French knight Robert of Boves, count of Amiens, had publicly repented of his long-standing refusal to pay an annual tax promised by his predecessors to the monastery of St Acheul in Amiens. Arrangements such as this also had spiritual dimensions, for Henry left money to pay for annual Masses to be said for himself and his family by the nuns.

By the late thirteenth century, crusaders were serving for pay from kings and other noble leaders. This reflected a societal shift away from raising armies through traditional customary service and towards the contractual hiring of troops for specific campaigns. In part this came about because the European nobility wanted to have a say in when and under what circumstances their kings went to war. By the 1270s, King Edward I of England could only make war when Parliament granted him the right to raise taxes to do so – otherwise he had to borrow huge sums privately. In 1270, when he led a crusading expedition to the Holy Land, he was already making contractual arrangements with knights, such as that which kept Adam of Jesmond and his four followers in royal service for a year for the sum of six hundred marks. Naturally, kings themselves could only mobilize armies made up of knights like Adam if they could lay their hands on large supplies of cash. In the second half of the thirteenth century, it became standard practice for kings to be allowed by popes to tax the clergy in their own realms specifically for this purpose, for a period of years before leaving on crusade. The expectation that had governed crusade recruitment for 150 years, that is, that crusades would be financed largely by the incremental contributions of thousands of individual participating knights, was over.

Assuming that a crusader had succeeded in raising whatever sums he could in ready capital, the next task was to co-ordinate his departure with others. How this was achieved in early crusading enterprises is still largely a matter of guesswork, but it is likely that small groups from the same localities set out together for major centres – for example, the court of a feudal magnate who was known to be assembling an army. On the Second (1147–9) and Third (1189–92) Crusades, co-ordination was easier because these expeditions were led by kings, and the machinery of royal government in England, France and the Holy Roman Empire could be put at the disposal of the crusade. In 1191, for example, Richard I assembled his crusade army in France and marched into Italy, where he had contracted with the Genoese to arrange passage by sea. Even when things went wrong on crusade, the presence of a king could facilitate a change of plan. When his army was left in tatters after bruising encounters with the Turks in Asia Minor in 1147, Louis VII was able to arrange shipping at short notice from the coastal town of Adana to Laodicea. Participants in the Fourth Crusade discovered in 1202 just how much could go wrong when travel was not co-ordinated. The decision of

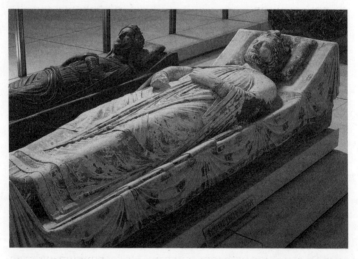

Figure 1   Tomb effigy of Richard the Lionheart, Fontevraud Abbey, Anjou. Richard was buried near his father Henry II, and, after her death in 1204, his mother Eleanor of Aquitaine was also buried here. (Source: Wikimedia Commons)

some groups of crusaders to make their own arrangements for departure without consulting the baronial council in charge of the leadership meant that all the planning work was wasted and that there was not enough money to pay for the shipping that had been contracted at Venice. Geoffrey de Villehardouin, one of the baronial leaders, wrote afterwards in his memoirs that this lack of co-ordination proved fatal to the success of the crusade.

Part of successful co-ordination was the ability to control large armies en route to their destination. The first crusaders (1096–1101) found this particularly difficult because no overall chain of command had been agreed before they set out. Crusaders pillaged and looted towns and villages in Hungary and the Balkans even before reaching 'enemy' territory, and, most notoriously, some groups of crusaders attacked Jewish communities in Normandy and in towns along the Rhine. By the mid-twelfth century, crusaders were regulating not only the direction of the routes but also the conduct of crusaders. This is implicit in Pope Eugenius III's crusading bull of 1145–6, and developed further in the *Capture of Lisbon,* an eyewitness account of one of the campaigns associated with the Second Crusade (1147–9). Measures were taken to ensure that the kind of loose behaviour usually associated with medieval armies on the march or on campaign – gambling, drunkenness, casual sex – was limited. Much of what was said about crusaders' behaviour by Raoul, the author of the *Capture of Lisbon,* shows the strong monastic influence behind these ideals, which included the expectation that crusaders would regularly attend Mass. Crusaders were reminded that they were not just ordinary soldiers, but pilgrims on the march. Henry II of England's 'Geddington Ordinances' (1188), disseminated after he had taken the cross for the Third Crusade, reinforced this sense of moral and spiritual obligation with royal authority. Heavy punishments were threatened for anyone caught stealing, or who committed violence against another crusader. When Richard I took over leadership of the Angevin crusade army, he added further stipulations about the disposal of the property of crusaders who died en route, so as to help destitute crusaders.

How crusaders travelled to the East changed dramatically in the third quarter of the twelfth century. Until then, the overland route was preferred because, although it was slow and sometimes dangerous, it enabled large armies to travel together and avoided the expense and uncertainty of sea voyages. For some crusaders from north-west Europe, such as the Norwegian expedition of 1107, the sea route was always the logical choice. But even on the short Adriatic sea crossing from Apulia to the Greek coast, a storm took the lives of many crusaders in 1096, and the pilgrim Saewulf could only watch helplessly as a number of ships unloading pilgrims were wrecked by a storm at Jaffa in 1102, while in 1254 Louis IX barely escaped with his life on return from the Holy Land when fire broke out on his ship. James of Vitry describes vividly his terror at being caught in a storm while en route from Genoa to Acre in 1216, in terms that would have been familiar to generations of crusaders:

> The front part of our ship was at one moment lifted up towards the stars, and at the next sunk into the depths. The storm lasted for two straight days and nights; some of our people could scarcely bear the violence of the wind, which brought down the ship's fo'c'sle, and broke down, while others refused food or drink for fear of dying. I did not eat any cooked food because we did not dare to light a fire on the ship.

> [Author's translation from *Lettres de Jacques de Vitry*, ed. R.B.C. Huygens (Leiden: Brill, 1960), pp. 79–97.]

The trauma of the mauling inflicted on German and French armies in Asia Minor in 1147, however, seemed to decide most future crusaders against the overland route. Emperor Frederick Barbarossa decided to take his army overland in 1189, perhaps because he wanted to exorcise his personal memory of 1147, but it proved his undoing because he died en route, and no subsequent crusade army until the fifteenth century tried it again. Shipping was more efficient and less risky by the late twelfth century, and because it was always much quicker to travel by sea, armies did not face the logistical problems of provisioning men and horses for such long periods. Even so, conditions could be nightmarish. Space was cramped – most ships transporting crusaders and pilgrims would only have had about 1,500 square feet of deck space, and only those of the highest rank would have had cabins of their own. Food and water were liable to go off very quickly, which meant that illness from food poisoning, added to seasickness, weakened crusading armies considerably.

The preparations for the Fourth Crusade also remind us how much forward planning went into transporting an army by sea. The Venetians signed a contract with the crusade leaders in 1200 to supply shipping for the army. They undertook to build enough ships to transport 4,500 knights with their horses, 9,000 squires and 20,000 foot soldiers. Venice was a great trading power, but its ruler, the doge, knew that it was not possible simply to put existing commercial vessels to the use of transporting an army. New ships had to be built, especially for transporting horses, so that when the army arrived at its destination they did not have to be lifted out by cranes, a lengthy and vulnerable process, but could walk or charge on to the beaches. Moreover, while the Venetian shipyards were employed in building these vessels, they would be unable to work on the mainstay of Venice's normal income, its trading ships. The sum demanded – 85,000 marks – was partly for materials and labour, and partly in compensation for lost commercial income.

Given the perils of travel to the theatre of war, many crusaders were probably in little condition to fight once they arrived. In fact, not all of them were expected to do so. The ranks of the first crusaders included many who went as non-combatant pilgrims, and some crusaders brought wives and families with them. All crusading armies also included clergy in their ranks, to reinforce the fact that these were no ordinary campaigns but holy wars. The clergy might take part in the fighting, despite increasing disapproval on the part of the Church of the shedding of blood by priests. In any case, there was plenty of work to be done on the march and in siege warfare that did not require actual fighting – helping with the sick and wounded, bringing up and distributing supplies, helping to build entrenched positions and siege engines, and so on.

Much of the business of war in the Middle Ages involved either manoeuvring for position or staying in the same place for long periods of time. Typically, a military campaign saw a good deal of getting armies from one place to another, if possible quicker than the enemy, either to secure food supplies or to deny the enemy access to them. It might involve destruction of property and crops on a large scale, some raiding and small-scale but violent action by small groups of opposing forces, and often inflicting misery on local populations. Pitched battles were rare – though possibly less so on crusades than in domestic warfare in the West, since commanders realized that in order to accomplish anything lasting they needed to engage the enemy as fully as possible.

More typical of crusader warfare were sieges. All the major crusades featured a siege against at least one fortified city. In the three hundred years following Pope Urban II's launch of the First Crusade in 1095, many of the major cities of the Mediterranean coastline and hinterland were besieged by crusading forces: Nicaea, Antioch, Jerusalem, Damascus, Constantinople, Damietta, Alexandria, Tunis, Tripoli, Acre, Lisbon, besides countless castles and fortifications. On the whole, the rate of success in siege warfare was better than in pitched battles, and the captures of Antioch (1097–8), Damietta (1219) and Constantinople (1203–4), for example, rank among the major military achievements of the period.

Siege warfare was liable to be time-consuming, expensive – both of manpower and money – and boring. As in the case of Acre

NAVAL SIEGE WARFARE

All of the major crusading expeditions involved besieging one or more fortified towns in the East. On the whole, with the exception of the siege of Damascus in 1148, the crusaders were successful in capturing towns by siege, though often (notably Antioch in the First Crusade, Acre in the Third and Damietta in the Fifth), only after sieges of several months' duration. Lisbon (1147), Acre (1189–91), Constantinople (1203–4) and Damietta (1218–19), all coastal towns, could only be taken through combined naval and land assaults. These operations demanded new technological solutions. At the siege of Constantinople, the Venetian galleys manouevred into position against the sea walls on the south side of the Bosphorus, having fixed long ladders that could swivel from the masts to reach the top of the walls, allowing soldiers to clamber on to them. During the siege of Damietta, the cleric Oliver of Cologne devised a siege engine mounted on a ship in order to attack a defensive tower located on a small island. The tower, from which a chain stretched across to the defensive walls of the town, was the key to gaining entry to the harbour, from which the crusader ships could attack the town's inner defences. At Acre, siege engines such as mangonels – huge catapults – were mounted on ships to hurl missiles at the sea walls. This was an operation requiring considerable seamanship, especially since the prevailing winds were liable to drive the ships towards the shore.

(1189–91) and Damietta (1218–19), a siege might last well over a year. During this period, crusaders obviously had to be supplied continually – as soon as the food ran out, the siege could no longer be continued. During the siege of Antioch in 1098, supplies ran so short that a small loaf of bread cost a bezant (i.e. a gold coin) and a single egg two shillings, and in the following winter, if contemporary chronicles are to be believed, crusaders resorted to cannibalism. Although careful commanders, like Louis IX in 1248–50, prepared the ground by sending ahead large supplies of cereals and barley, almost all crusaders must have experienced hunger at some point. Famine broke out during the sieges of Antioch on the First Crusade and of Acre on the Third. On several occasions during crusading expeditions knights were reduced to eating horseflesh, because it was too expensive to keep their mounts alive over winter when pasture was short. The response to such conditions was charity. By the spring of 1099, the first crusaders had agreed to pool the spoils of war so as to keep alive those who had run out of food and funds, but this measure followed an original policy of simply encouraging the 'haves' to be as charitable as possible to the 'have-nots'.

Diseases resulted from malnutrition, and, of course, it was much more difficult to prevent the spread of disease as a result of poor sanitation when the army was encamped – as all armies up to the twentieth century have found. Diphtheria and dysentery raged throughout encamped crusading armies, especially when they were forced to stop in unhealthy locations. Louis IX became too ill with dysentery in Egypt in 1250 to continue effective leadership, and many of the crusaders with him were attacked by scurvy – Joinville describes rather too vividly the treatment for those who were afflicted, as the diseased flesh around their gums was cut away. And, during the siege of Acre in 1191, both Richard I and Philip II suffered from bouts of illness, perhaps malaria.

If royal figures, who had more comfortable living conditions than most, could not stay healthy, there was little hope for the bulk of the crusaders. It was once assumed that Western medical practices and expertise lagged far behind those of the Arab world, but recent research suggests that the basis of practical knowledge was not so very different. It is probable that many battle and siege casualties died who could have been saved, because it was impossible to provide adequate basic first aid in the conditions of conflict. Just as in the fields of Flanders in 1914–18, many men probably bled to death from relatively treatable wounds because they could not be reached in time. On the other hand, life-threatening wounds could be healed in more peaceful conditions. Godfrey of Bouillon suffered a severed artery while fighting a bear during the First Crusade, but the wound was cauterized and he survived.

Given the pattern of military activity on crusade, many crusaders had a good deal of time on their hands. The First, Third and Fifth Crusades (1096–9, 1189–92 and 1217–21) occupied upwards of three years, even if on the two latter expeditions arrivals and departures were staggered. Even Louis IX's first crusade (1248–50), which was one of the best-organized, saw a striking imbalance between action and either marching or waiting around in camp. Initial arrival in Cyprus was followed by months of preparation, waiting for reinforcements and for a change in weather before the army set sail for its Egyptian destination. Once at Damietta, there was a brief flurry of action as the almost deserted town was captured, then a further period of delay while the army waited for the Nile floods to subside so that manoeuvring was possible. The main action of the crusade took place over a period of about twelve weeks from November to February 1249–50, but the principal military encounter took place on a single day – 8 February – after which a prolonged period of negotiating and uncertainty set in. Finally, Louis left Egypt in April 1250, but most of his army remained in captivity for several months after that. On the Second Crusade, the armies took three months to march from Constantinople to the south coast of Asia Minor, during which they were under heavy attack much of the time. Once in the Crusader States, however, between March and November 1148, the period of military action was scarcely a week, during the humiliating siege of Damascus.

It is hardly surprising, given this pattern of inactivity, that clerical commentators found plenty to concern them in the daily conduct of crusaders. Gambling, foul language and sexual licence were, if we are to credit the clergy, the main preoccupations of crusaders. There seems to have been plenty of opportunity for casual sex during crusades. During the siege of Antioch on the First Crusade, a priest was told by Jesus in a vision that the reason the crusaders had become bogged down was that their sexual conduct was far from what was expected of pilgrims, and at one point on the same expedition a man and woman found committing adultery were stripped naked and marched round all the crusaders' camps while being publicly beaten with sticks. On the Fifth Crusade, during the army's long delay at Damietta (1219–21), prostitutes were whipped and branded with hot irons. James of Vitry, our source for this piece of information, was highly critical of the crusaders' behaviour at Damietta, blaming the stalling of the crusade on their idleness and lack of serious-mindedness, but it was unrealistic to expect an army to behave like monks, and the lack of progress of the crusade was not the fault of ordinary crusaders but of a dysfunctional leadership. Reviewing the events of the First Crusade a few years after it had finished, Fulcher of Chartres, who had accompanied the army as a chaplain, wrote admiringly of the sense of solidarity on crusade. People who spoke different languages made themselves understood to one another, and if anyone lost anything it was restored to him rather than being stolen. Fulcher's idealized view was not borne out by the experience of most crusades. On the Second Crusade, the French crusaders' distrust of their (mostly French) hosts in the kingdom of Jerusalem seriously undermined the crusade itself, and on the Third Crusade relations between French and English crusaders broke down even before they reached the East. Perhaps ironically, it was on the Fourth Crusade (1202–4), which suffered more than most from weak leadership, that the different national contingents of crusaders – mostly northern French and Venetian – were best able to get on together.

Whatever the measure of success on a crusade, most crusaders wanted above all to return home alive. Even on the First Crusade, which more than any other was seen by contemporaries as an opportunity to conquer and settle new lands, only a fraction of crusaders stayed behind in the East. Crusading as an activity was more frequent than the traditional numbered expeditions would appear to suggest, because, in addition to these, there were countless individual crusading enterprises that took the form of armed pilgrimages undertaken by smaller groups of knights without reference to specific papal preaching. Only in a very few cases can we infer that crusaders or pilgrims intended to settle in the East. Given this pattern, surprisingly little attention has been paid to the circumstances and practicalities of returning home. Knights who had left with high hopes might return with serious wounds or infirmities and find it difficult to take up their former way of life with the same vigour. Others found that lands they had thought safe in the hands of relatives or under the nominal protection of the Church were plundered or attacked while they were away; wives or heirs had died; harvests failed; and property had been sold to keep things going. Knights who had taken the cross in the hope of becoming rich were largely disappointed; there is very little evidence of crusaders returning home wealthier than when they had left. In less tangible ways, however, crusading conferred huge benefits on crusaders who survived to tell the tale. Even if their expedition had failed, they were heroic figures whose devotion to the cross would be rewarded in the afterlife and whose prestige in their community increased immeasurably. Crusaders are described in many chronicles in terms of respect and awe. Whether they had been changed emotionally or spiritually by their experiences is much harder to know. The author of the contemporary biography of King Louis VI of France describes the career of one of the most lawless barons in the kingdom, Thomas of Marle, in terms that make him appear to have been devoid of any human sentiment. As one historian has remarked, it is something of a surprise to realize that he was a crusader, whose exploits on the First Crusade earned him a reputation for piety and chivalry.

3

The First Crusade

The First Crusade was a voyage into the unknown. Many of the humbler crusaders – peasants or the urban poor – had probably never been more than a few miles from the places of their birth, and among the better travelled, only a small handful would have had first-hand experience of the landscapes of the eastern Mediterranean. The journey had to be undertaken largely by land, much of it through hostile territory. Supplying troops and horses, and maintaining or replacing worn equipment, had to be done from the resources of the lands through which the crusaders passed. Most crusaders probably ran out of their own money long before they reached Turkish-held lands, which meant that supplies could no longer be bought but had to be plundered, even from local populations who were themselves Christian. Even the crusade leaders probably had little idea of what kind of military strength they would have to face, or even how to get to Jerusalem. Logistically, the crusade posed challenges the like of which had never been faced before by European armies.

There was no central organization or command structure in the early stages of the crusade. Armies formed under the banners of the great lords – in the north of France, Robert, duke of Normandy, Robert, count of Flanders, and Stephen, count of Blois; in German-speaking regions, the three brothers of the Bouillon-Ardennes dynasty, Eustace, count of Boulogne, Godfrey, duke of Lower Lotharingia, and their younger brother Baldwin; in the south of France, Raymond of Saint-Gilles, count of Toulouse, who was accompanied by the pope's own representative, Adhemar, bishop of Le Puy. Many of the recruits were already vassals of these great lords, and participation was probably largely determined by political, social and family relationships. Great lords exercised political power through patronage, and in a small society access to them could be surprisingly direct. But there were also crusaders who had no prior relationship with the crusade leaders and who gathered under their banners because they represented the leadership of their region. The expedition also gathered momentum as it passed through lands where Urban's message had not been preached. In southern Italy, Normans had created a patchwork of lordships in the two generations since they first settled there in the 1030s. Competition for land and resources was intense. Bohemond, son of the great Robert Guiscard, who had made Apulia his own, was battling to secure his father's inheritance against his stepbrother when he heard about the crusade from contingents on their way to the Apulian ports. Gathering an army of his own, he took the cross and set off for the East.

Although the different crusade armies relied on their own initiative in setting out, it seems to have been agreed that they would meet at Constantinople. After all, it was partly at the urging of the emperor that the expedition was taking place at all, and the crusaders knew that they would be crossing territory that had until recently been Byzantine, and in which the population was still Greek-speaking and Greek Orthodox. Only when they crossed the Litani in Lebanon would they be in lands where the majority of the population was Arab and where memories of Byzantine rule were more than twenty years distant.

The first armies to reach Constantinople, however, were not at all what the Byzantine emperor, Alexios Komnenos, had intended. Fired by enthusiastic preaching, groups of crusaders had already left with Peter the Hermit in advance of the main crusade leaders, taking a route along the Rhine and Danube towards the heart of the Byzantine Empire. These groups, often – rather

THE BYZANTINE EMPIRE

In the fifth century, after the collapse of Roman power in the West, the seat of the Empire shifted to the eastern Mediterranean. Constantine's new capital, Constantinople, became the centre of government over the prosperous east Roman provinces: Greece, Asia Minor, Syria, Palestine and Egypt. The Arab invasions of the seventh century, however, meant that by c.700, Egypt, Syria and Palestine had been lost to the Empire, and in the eleventh century much of Asia Minor was lost to the Seljuq Turks, while the Empire's northern borders were threatened by the rise of the Bulgar kingdom. The Byzantine state was based on the supreme position of the emperor, supported by a sophisticated civil service. Although Constantinople itself continued to impress western visitors, including crusaders, with its magnificent public buildings and churches, and Byzantine culture, artistic techniques and craftsmanship were highly prized, the Empire during the period of the Crusades faced slow decline, especially after the capture of Constantinople by the Fourth Crusade (1204). Although Greek was the language of the Byzantine Empire, its inhabitants called themselves *Rhomaioi* ('Romans') until the final fall of the Empire to the Ottomans in 1453, to emphasize the fact that they were the heirs to the Romans.

misleadingly – called the Popular Crusade, were more difficult to control than the main armies because their leaders had neither the political authority nor the resources to do so. Although led by knights and clerics, they comprised largely peasants and urban poor, and many were probably non-combatants. Groups of Germans, French and Flemish under the leadership of Count Emicho of Leiningen, Count Hartmann of Dilingen and Drogo of Nesle caused the first human tragedies of the crusade by turning on the defenceless Jewish communities of Rhineland towns. Appalling violence was perpetrated on the Jews of Speyer, Trier,

Metz, Cologne, Worms, Mainz and Regensburg. Jews were humili-
ated, robbed, tortured and killed, in some cases having conversion
forced on them at the point of the sword. It is not clear how
many casualties there were, because the total number of Jews
in these towns cannot be estimated accurately. What is certain
is the horror that this episode caused among the Jews – horror
that still lives in the words of the contemporary chroniclers. In
Mainz, for example, Emicho of Leiningen and a band of crusaders
besieged the Jews of the town in the palace of the archbishop,
where they had taken refuge. Once they had broken through
the flimsy defences, they slaughtered men, women and children,
some of the Jewish families killing themselves first rather than be
subjected to the violence of the mob. This was the first, though
tragically not the last time that organized brutality of this kind
resulted from religious zeal in Christian Europe. The preaching
of crusades in 1147 and 1190 was also accompanied by similar
acts of violence against Jewish communities. In some cases the
violence seems to have been perpetrated simply to rob Jews or,
in 1190 in York, to destroy evidence of indebtedness to Jews. But
not all Jews were wealthy, and in any case the levels of violence
went beyond what was necessary to accomplish simple robbery.
We can only conclude that, in the hands of some preachers of the
crusade and their audiences, the message of just war against the
Turkish occupiers of the Holy Land was distorted into violence
against all non-Christians.

Emperor Alexios must have been dismayed at the sight of these
first crusaders. Penniless by the time they reached Constantinople,
they were fractious and disrespectful, and Alexios shipped them
across the Bosphorus to Asia Minor as soon as possible in August
1096. They quickly attracted the attention of the Seljuqs by
plundering the region around Civetot, and in October the entire
remaining force of about five hundred knights and several thousand
foot soldiers was soundly defeated. The first wave of the crusade
had ended in disaster.

Over the next six months, the main armies arrived and were welcomed by Alexios. It was here that the strategy to be followed by the crusade was hatched. Alexios re-equipped the armies and offered money to the leaders. Not all accepted, however, for Alexios also required the leaders to take an oath of loyalty to him. Quite what the oath signified to the emperor or to the crusaders is unclear, partly because the contemporary accounts contradict one another. During the course of the crusade, the relationship between crusaders and Byzantines was to turn sour, and most of the chroniclers, whose reports were of course all compiled with the benefit of hindsight, no longer wanted to present Alexios in the light in which he probably appeared to the crusaders at the time – as a generous benefactor. Raymond of Toulouse and Bohemond's nephew Tancred both refused to take the oath, but most of the leaders saw that they had no choice. Bohemond may indeed have seen it as a way of building a new career in the East. The former Byzantine territories that Alexios expected the crusaders to reconquer would need to be governed and guarded by someone on the spot with a strong military presence, and Bohemond and some of the other crusade leaders who did not have extensive lands waiting for them at home knew that the Byzantines often took capable foreigners into imperial service.

The crusaders' first objective was the Byzantine town of Nicaea, near the eastern coast of the Sea of Marmora, which the Seljuq sultan Kilij Arslan had fortified as a regional capital. The five-week siege, in May and June 1097, was the first taste of war against the Turks for most crusaders. It was also their first experience of dealing with the Byzantines as allies. Alexios had sent an army led by the half-Arab general Tatikios to fight alongside the crusaders and guide them through Asia Minor. The combined crusader forces proved too much for the small garrison, and Kilij Arslan, having mistakenly taken Peter the Hermit's force for the main crusade army, arrived back in the area too late to be able to save the situation and withdrew after being driven from the field. Some of the contemporary chronicles report crusaders grumbling at being deprived of the chance to plunder in the town, but Alexios had no intention of letting the Greek population suffer a sack and discipline held. It had been a deceptively comfortable beginning for the crusaders in contrast to what they were to confront over the next two years.

It was probably already decided that the next objective would be Antioch, the largest city in the eastern Mediterranean and one with a predominantly Greek and Armenian population. It had been reconquered from the Abbasid caliphate in 969 and remained in Byzantine hands until 1086; its recapture was the necessary corner-stone of Alexios' attempt to restore imperial fortunes in the East. As they set off across Anatolia, the crusaders probably numbered about 70,000 to 75,000 in total, but of these only about 7,500 would have been mounted knights. The rest were foot soldiers, as well as the essential support staff for any army, including cooks, carpenters, armourers and servants. Many were women, and some crusaders had brought their families with them. The total strength probably also included unarmed pilgrims. A force of this size was unwieldy and could not live off the land, so the crusaders split into two forces. Once again taking half the force for the whole, Kilij Arslan trapped and surrounded the Normans and south Italians. It was a close shave until the second army arrived and chased the Turks from the field. For about five hours, the crusade looked doomed, since there was no prospect of escape for the armies led by Robert of Normandy and Bohemond. It was an expensive victory, with perhaps as many as 4,000 crusader casualties, but much had been gained. Kilij Arslan had been effectively dealt with as a threat to the crusade's progress; he gave no more trouble.

Equally important, perhaps, the crusaders had faced the Turks in open battle and now knew how they could be defeated. Typically, Turkish armies relied on speed and mobility, using massed cavalry archers to great effect. Their horses were more manoeuvrable than the Franks', but both their cavalry and infantry could be dispersed by the greater weight of a Frankish cavalry charge. Western warfare had by the 1090s developed a distinctive technology. Huge horses of 15–16 hands were bred and trained for war: carrying knights fully armed in knee-length tunics of interlocking metal chains, they were themselves aggressive weapons launched in charges of high speed. Against infantry, or cavalry on smaller horses, they could trample and kick an enemy brutally. The knights wielded lances as long as fourteen feet couched under the arm. The purpose of the cavalry charge was to disperse an enemy by weight of iron and momentum. But the tactic only worked when there was enough space available to launch the charge; in restricted spaces, the advantages of weight and speed were lost as horses and men became tangled and knights could be isolated from their companions. It was also a form of warfare in which the advantage relied on the technology of the warhorse. With every engagement the crusaders fought, they lost horses, and such fresh ones as could be found in Asia Minor and Syria were not of the same size or weight. Horses also needed pasture or fodder, and as the winter came on this would become an insurmountable problem.

The armies split again in eastern Asia Minor. In a pincer movement, two small contingents under Baldwin and Tancred were dispatched to secure the towns of Cilicia, whose population was mainly Armenian and likely to support the crusaders, while the main armies pushed eastward to Caesarea, where the passes in the Anti-Taurus mountain range were large enough to accommodate them. Baldwin entangled himself in the local politics of the Armenians of north Syria and engineered control of the town of Edessa, which became the first long-term Frankish conquest of the crusade. But Antioch would present more serious challenges than these adventures. The crusader armies reached it in autumn 1097 and prepared for a long siege. The main problem at first was that the city could not be surrounded totally, partly because the crusaders did not have forces large enough to stretch around the five-kilometre extent of the walls, and partly because the city straggled over the heights of Mount Silpius, which presented an impossible barrier to the east for a besieging army as long as the citadel remained in the hands of the garrison. Besides this, the largest extent of flat terrain, on the west side of the city, was partly protected by the river Orontes.

ANTIOCH

Antioch, one of the great urban centres of the ancient world, was still an important city when the crusaders captured it from the Turks in 1098. Having only been in Turkish hands since 1086, its population was largely still Greek-speaking, though the Armenian migrations to south-east Asia Minor and the Euphrates basin had also brought a substantial Armenian population by c.1100. Under the Norman rule of Bohemond, Tancred and Roger of Salerno, Antioch developed as a pluralistic society in which political and governmental customs imported from the new rulers' homeland of southern Italy operated alongside local customs. The Principality of Antioch expanded to encompass large parts of north Syria and some of the cities of Cilicia, in south-east Asia Minor. In 1119, however, the Antiochenes suffered a crushing defeat at the hands of Il-Ghazi at the battle of the Field of Blood, and this initiated a period in which the principality became dependent on military support from the kingdom of Jerusalem. Although Antioch was not conquered by Saladin in 1187, in the thirteenth century its rulers had to contend with the increasing power of the Armenian kings of Cilicia. Relations with the local Greek population also became strained, and in the early thirteenth century the Frankish ruler had to contend with a hostile commune. By the mid-thirteenth century, in order to guarantee its survival, Antioch had become part of a nexus of alliances with the Mongols as well as the Armenians; even so, it was conquered by Baibars in 1268 and almost totally destroyed.

Unable either to starve out the garrison or to storm the walls, the crusaders had no choice but to suffer near-starvation in the wet north-Syrian winter. Meanwhile, their presence had attracted attention. Besides the obduracy of the Turkish garrison, they had to fend off three separate attacks from Seljuq armies. The first, sent by Duqaq, the emir of Damascus, was intercepted before it reached Antioch to raise the siege, but a second, led by Ridwan, the emir of Aleppo, had to be fought off in a desperate battle in February 1098 at the Iron Bridge, the main crossing point of the Orontes, twelve miles north of Antioch. This was Bohemond's triumph. Having left the infantry at Antioch to maintain the siege, he led a force of no more than 1,000 mounted knights to meet Ridwan. Persuading the other leaders to follow his strategy, he boldly divided his army in the face of superior odds – as many as 12:1 – into six mobile units. With the advantage of surprise and brilliant use of heavy cavalry, five units engaged the vanguard while Bohemond waited for the ideal moment to charge at Ridwan as his huge army squeezed together to cross the bridge. It was a complete victory that gave the crusaders breathing space until the spring could bring better weather and thus fresh supplies from the west. With the arrival of an English supply fleet at the port of St Symeon in March, the crusaders now had food as well as timber to build siege engines. At last they could mount a serious assault on the walls.

Even so, it took something unexpected to break the siege. In mid-May, Bohemond managed to bribe the commander of a section of the southern walls near the St George gate to betray the city. This man, Firuz, was an Armenian, probably a Muslim convert. On a night in early June, a party of crusaders led by Bohemond was allowed to climb rope ladders over the walls while Firuz's men not only stood by but opened a postern gate for a larger force to enter. By morning, the city was in the crusaders' hands. However, the dramatic climax to the capture of Antioch was still to come. The city was theirs, but the citadel remained in the hands of the garrison. A day later, a fresh Seljuq army arrived, led by Kerbogha of Mosul, the most powerful Turkish emir in Syria. With an army large enough to surround the city, and the advantage of being in possession of the citadel, which provided access from the heights of Mount Silpius, he must have thought he could finish off the crusaders. Certainly some crusaders thought so. One of the crusade leaders, Stephen, count of Blois, had already deserted before Bohemond's suborning of Firuz; others slipped away as the cordon tightened around them. But once again, a combination of military skill and a will to prevail – which we might call faith – proved irresistible. Bohemond, again, deserves the credit. After three days of fasting and processions from the ancient churches of Antioch, the crusaders burst out of the city in four distinct contingents based on national groupings – northern French, Germans and Lotharingians, southern French and south Italians – to confront Kerbogha head-on. They were now principally an infantry force, having lost most of their horses, and probably numbered no more than around 20,000 men. But the boldness of their battle plan threw Kerbogha into confusion, and he first missed his chance to bottle the crusaders up before they could leave the city in battle order, and then mistimed his attempt to gather together his besieging forces. Despite his vastly superior numbers, he was unable to maintain control of his army and was forced to flee. Antioch had been won.

One of the casualties of the Antioch campaign was the Byzantine alliance. The crusaders considered that the emperor had broken his word by abandoning them to the siege without reinforcements, and Bohemond seized for himself the city that he had done so much to conquer. It is likely that Alexios would have sent some reinforcements had he considered it worthwhile, but communication with the crusaders had been lost once they were beyond the Taurus mountains, and the latest intelligence he had of them came from Stephen of Blois, who stopped in Constantinople on his way back home to announce that Kerbogha's arrival meant all was lost. From now on, the crusaders were on their own, but the failure of the alliance was to have serious consequences for the future.

The crusade lost momentum after the victory, and it was not until the new year of 1099 that a reduced force – without Bohemond, who stayed in Antioch – made its way south along the coast toward Jerusalem. This delay has given rise to some speculation about the crusaders' real intentions. Had they all intended to go as far as Jerusalem, or had the recovery of Antioch, in response to the Byzantine appeal at Piacenza in 1095, been the ultimate objective? In any case, it was now that Raymond of Saint-Gilles came into his own, shepherding the pilgrim army south. Raymond had lost credibility as a leader among the crusaders in comparison with Bohemond's decisive military leadership. Now, with Bohemond refusing to leave his new city, Raymond took charge of the crusaders. There was no resistance to speak of once they had moved into the backwaters that were Palestine in the 1090s. While the crusaders were besieging Antioch, southern Palestine, including Jerusalem itself, had been taken by the Fatimid caliphate of Egypt, and much of the former Roman province was a no man's land in which no real lordship existed. Jerusalem itself was a different matter. High on the fringe of cultivable land, far from trade routes, with arid semi-desert to the south and east, and no natural water supply, territorially and economically unimportant it may have been, but as numerous armies were to find over the centuries, it was easy to defend and difficult to crack.

In order to take any walled city by force, a besieging army needed supplies of wood, rope and tools to build siege towers, ladders and engines that could throw projectiles. Only when a fleet of six Genoese ships carrying building equipment and crafts-men arrived at Jaffa could the crusaders really begin the siege in earnest, helped by local Christians who showed them where wood could be found. By the time the assault on Jerusalem began, relations among the leaders were desperately bad. Raymond of

Figure 2 Bronze statue of Godfrey of Bouillon in the Hofkirche, Innsbruck, sixteenth century. The enduring popularity of Godfrey as a Christian chivalric hero continued into the Reformation period. (Source: Wikimedia Commons)

Saint-Gilles' authority had diminished because of his support for the Provencal priest Peter Bartholomew. In Antioch, at the critical moment before the final battle against Kerbogha, Peter had claimed to have been shown in a vision the location of the holy lance – the spear that had pierced Christ's side at the Crucifixion. Although the pilgrim army was certainly predisposed to believe that such relics could be found, and that, if genuine, they were powerful signs of God's favour, they did not invariably accept them as genuine. This was the case with the holy lance. Even when Peter produced what he said was the relic, the other crusade leaders suspected that Raymond had manipulated the whole affair in order to advance his credit with the army, at a time when Bohemond's stock was high. But, given that the odds against their survival at Antioch were poor, Raymond may have thought that the crusaders would be willing to grasp at any straw. In any case, the affair was not forgotten, and while the crusaders were struggling under Raymond's command to take Arqa on the march south to Jerusalem, Peter Bartholomew was required to undergo a trial by ordeal to prove the genuineness of the relic. He walked through an inferno carrying the relic wrapped in a cloth, but when he died of his wounds a few days later, it was his patron Raymond's credibility that plummeted. Now, at Jerusalem, Raymond found himself stuck on the south side of the city, where the walls plunged down into the Valley of Hinnom, while Godfrey of Bouillon and Tancred assembled their siege towers on the north side of the city, where the ground was level.

It was Godfrey's contingent that broke through the defences and stormed the walls first, on 15 July 1099. There followed days of bloodletting, presented by some of the chroniclers as a ritual cleansing of the city. It is difficult to reconstruct the events with accuracy, but there is little doubt that large numbers of inhabitants, including Jews and native Christians as well as Muslims, and non-combatants as well as the Egyptian garrison, were massacred and the city systematically looted. It was an atrocity that made a lasting impact on the Islamic world.

Against all reasonable expectations, the crusade had succeeded in its military objective – but at an appalling cost. Perhaps only ten percent of the knighthood that had left the fields and green valleys of western Europe survived to celebrate the victory in the heat and dust of Judaea. The crusade had made the reputations of some great lords, such as Godfrey of Bouillon and Tancred, the fortunes of a few others, notably Baldwin and Bohemond, and destroyed the careers of yet others, such as Stephen of Blois and Raymond of Saint-Gilles. The victors had prevailed through a combination of their own military skill and determination, but also because of mistakes made by the Seljuq commanders, Kilij Arslan, Ridwan and Kerbogha. Any of these three could – and should – have halted the crusade in its tracks, but none was able to grasp the nature of a kind of warfare that was new to them. Godfrey's hold over the new conquest of Jerusalem was secured by the defeat he and the surviving crusaders dealt out to an Egyptian army at Ascalon in August. The holy city was safe; now the crusaders needed to decide what to do with it.

4

The kingdom of Jerusalem

Most of the survivors of the First Crusade wanted to go back
to their homes. A small number, however, decided to stay on in
the Holy Land, either out of a pious desire to protect the Holy
Sepulchre or because they had nothing much to return to and
would rather make their fortunes in the East. They probably
numbered only a few hundred knights and foot soldiers, with a
smattering of clerics. They settled initially in and around Jerusalem,
Bethlehem and Jaffa under the leadership of Godfrey of Bouillon.
Gradually, as more territory came under their sway, they began
to colonize more and more land. We may well ask how so few
knights managed to create a kingdom in a short space of time and
with so few resources. One answer is that there was no effective
local opposition. Although the Fatimid caliph in Cairo and the
emir of Damascus periodically sent armies to dislodge them, there
was no military or political force to oppose them in the newly
conquered territory.

Palestine before 1098 was a patchwork of local landowners
and their dependent peasants in the countryside, who paid taxes
to the Seljuq governor but were largely powerless to determine
who actually ruled over them. There was also a number of towns
of varying size, the most economically important of which lay
on the coast. The Fatimid conquest of Jerusalem and southern
Palestine in 1098 was too recent for the Egyptians to have established a proper regime. The crusaders simply took over ownership

of such land and property as they could, leaving the peasants to continue working the land under new masters. Another reason is that there must have been steady immigration from the West in the decade or so after 1099. We know very little about the numbers or circumstances, but it is possible that many of the new arrivals came from southern Italy. By about 1110, the kingdom of Jerusalem was able to call on armies of about 500–600 mounted knights on occasion – probably more than twice the number that originally settled in Jerusalem.

What made the new Frankish settlement in the East viable was the capture of the coastal towns. It was the income from trade flowing through the ports that provided the king with the wealth he needed to retain enough knights to maintain a military force. Jaffa had fallen during the First Crusade; Haifa followed in 1101 and Acre in 1104, Beirut in 1109 and Sidon a year later, but Tyre was to fall only in 1124. The towns were not simply captured, but also depopulated. Muslim inhabitants were either forced into exile or resettled in the interior as agricultural labour – sometimes having been enslaved first. In some cases, where towns had resisted, the defenders were massacred. The towns thus became non-Muslim preserves, open only to Franks and indigenous Christians.

The ability of the first settlers not only to survive but also to expand into new territory was remarkable. By 1118, the kingdom of Jerusalem extended from the Negev desert in the south to the Litani river (Lebanon) in the north, and from the Mediterranean coast in the west to the desert east of the Jordan. In the 1120s attempts would even be made to conquer Damascus. The kingdom was the creation not of Godfrey of Bouillon, who died without heirs in 1100, but of his younger brother, Baldwin, who had marched south from Edessa immediately on hearing news of Godfrey's death. Baldwin's reign, though successful in many respects, was to prove typically unfortunate in one – the failure of the king to provide an heir. On Baldwin's death, also heirless, it was his cousin, Baldwin of Le Bourcq, a first crusader who had succeeded him in Edessa, who took the throne as Baldwin II. But Baldwin II, who had married an Armenian, only had daughters rather than sons, and this meant that the whole dynamic of power in the kingdom of Jerusalem shifted. A husband had to be found for the eldest, Melisende, if the royal line were to continue. A marriage alliance with the Byzantine imperial house was out of the question, for it would place the new kingdom in a subordinate position. On the other hand, marriage to one of the other Frankish baronial families who had settled in the East was not a particularly attractive prospect for the royal house. Because most of the great lords had returned home in 1099, those who remained to settle new lands tended to be those who had least to lose at home: lesser knights with no experience of lordship and no wealth of their own. By the 1120s, an 'upper class' among this baronage was emerging, but marriage to one of these would have provided no advantage to the kingdom. On the other hand, importing a husband for Melisende from the West would be a means of establishing links to a noble dynasty, with all the potential military advantages that might bring. In the event, the man chosen was Fulk V, count of Anjou. Already the father of an heir old enough to rule Anjou himself, Fulk had been on pilgrimage to Jerusalem and was willing to live there permanently. He married Melisende in 1129. She, like most nobly born women, had no choice in the matter: the priority was the future of the kingdom, not her happiness.

Fulk was a new type of crusader. He had first come to the Holy Land in 1120 on an armed pilgrimage; in other words, on a private crusade with a small contingent of knights from Anjou. This was already a common phenomenon by this period: even King Sigurd of Norway had done the same in 1109–10. The First Crusade had been a one-off event, but Western knights saw no reason why they should not continue to emulate the crusaders even without specific papal mandate. Jerusalem might have been in Christian hands, but there was still plenty of fighting to be done to defend the Holy Land, and since it was the same just cause for which an indulgence had been granted by Urban II, knights hoped for the same spiritual rewards. So there were significant numbers of 'unofficial' crusaders in the early years of the Crusader States – knights who wanted to make a pilgrimage to Jerusalem, but who followed the example set by the first crusaders and, rather than going unarmed and in poverty, offered their swords to the service of the kingdom. The evidence of chroniclers who wrote

THE PATRIARCHS OF JERUSALEM

The office of patriarch was an honorary title conferred by the early Church on bishoprics thought to have an especially distinguished Christian history. There were only five in the whole of Christendom: Rome, the see of St Peter; Constantinople, evangelized by St Andrew and the seat of the Roman Empire from the fourth century onward; Antioch, in Christian tradition the first place where St Peter preached; Alexandria, the see of St Mark and an important centre of the early Church; and Jerusalem itself. In the Western Catholic Church, the title of patriarch was merely honorific, and popes were usually known as bishops of Rome rather than patriarchs. In the Greek Orthodox Church, however, the title was important because an Ecumenical Council of the Church could only be called if all five patriarchs were present, and only an Ecumenical Council could determine Christian doctrine. After the First Crusade, the Western settlers took over the running of the Church in the lands they had conquered and retained the titles of patriarch for the bishoprics of Jerusalem and Antioch. The patriarch of Jerusalem was a major property owner in the city and throughout the Holy Land by virtue of his office. Even after the loss of Jerusalem in 1187, patriarchs continued to be appointed to Jerusalem by the Latin Church, though they resided in Acre until 1291.

about the kingdom of Jerusalem in the first twenty years of its existence – principally Fulcher of Chartres and Albert of Aachen – shows that although we know the names of only a handful of these, the regular annual presence of such 'private crusaders' was vital to the military activities of the kingdom.

Just before Fulk's first pilgrimage to the Holy Land, another initiative had helped to improve the military capability of the kingdom. In 1119, a group of unarmed pilgrims had been way-laid and massacred by local bandits on their way to the river Jordan, near Jericho, to worship at the site of Jesus' baptism. In response, a knight from Champagne, Hugh de Payens, had the idea of setting up a service that could provide a military escort for pilgrims. From this grew the Order of Knights of the Temple, so called because King Baldwin II gave them the royal palace in the al-Aqsa mosque on the Temple Mount in Jerusalem to serve as their headquarters. Some historians believe that the first Templars were knights who had remained behind after 1099 and entered the service of the head of the Church in the new kingdom, the patriarch of Jerusalem, and that, as this group expanded, they took on a wider range of military duties. They may have num-bered only thirty knights in 1119, but in 1129, at the Council of Troyes, the Templars were recognized by the pope as a distinct Order in the Church and adopted a quasi-monastic Rule. This was probably the result of a new recruitment drive in the West. The main centre of recruitment was northern France, especially Hugh's own region of Champagne. The count, Hugh, even gave up his title, family and property to join the Templars, and by 1131 their fame had spread so far that the king of Aragon, Alfonso the Battler, willed his kingdom jointly to the Templars, Hospitallers and the Holy Sepulchre. Further support for the Templars came from the influential abbot of Clairvaux, Bernard, whose uncle was Master of the Order. Bernard's treatise *In Praise of the New Knighthood* publicized their role in the defence of the Holy Land and promoted them as 'perfect knights', whose conduct and standards made them a cut above ordinary knights. Bernard praised their moderation, their sobriety, and their dedication to their cause. He saw them as 'monastic knights', the counterparts to monks in the sacrifices they made for the Holy Land. Templars gave up everything they had in their previous lives: when they joined the Templars they started at the bottom of the heap. They were like monks in that they took vows of poverty, obedience and celibacy; if they were married, they had to abandon wife and family and live in communal commanderies with their new brothers. The Rule of the Templars, which was added to over the course of the next hundred years, laid down how knights were to be organized in peace and war. Obedience to the officers of the Order was paramount for maintaining discipline, and infractions were penalized heavily. Templar knights were required to help one another on the battlefield, for example by picking up brothers whose horses had been killed under them, and were forbidden to leave the battlefield while a Templar banner was still standing, even if it meant certain capture or death. It is not surprising that the Templars were regarded as the most fanatical of enemies by Arab chroniclers.

The other major Military Order in the Crusader States had a less obvious military origin. The Hospital of St John took on military functions only after a generation or so of existence as a hospital in Jerusalem. The Hospital was founded in obscure circumstances at some point in the last twenty years of the eleventh century by a group of pious merchants from Amalfi, in southern Italy, who had come to Jerusalem on pilgrimage and been struck by the fate of pilgrims unfortunate enough to fall ill while in the East. Like all medieval hospitals, this was what we would call a hospice as much as a hospital, and it was run by a monastery, also founded by the Amalfitans, known as St Mary of the Latins. During the crusader siege of Jerusalem in 1099, the administrator of the hospital, Gerard, was tortured by the Fatimid defenders of the city, and once the city had fallen into

Frankish hands, his and the hospital's reputation swelled. The hospital received patronage in the form of cash gifts, property and bequests from both Godfrey of Bouillon and Baldwin I, and by 1114 it was powerful and wealthy enough to be recognized by the papacy as an autonomous institution. Pilgrims to Jerusalem described the size and efficiency of the hospital, which had a thousand beds, in awestruck terms. The hospital first seems to have taken on military functions in the 1130s. In 1136, King Fulk reinforced the southern frontiers of the kingdom of Jerusalem by building a series of castles to contain any possible attack from Egypt. One of these, Beth Gibelin, was entrusted to the Hospitallers. At first, they probably hired mercenary soldiers to garrison it, but fairly quickly the members of the Order seem to have merged the functions of nursing the sick and manning castles. Like the Templars, Hospitaller Knights took vows that were monastic in character and had to dedicate themselves to religious lives.

By 1148, when both Orders took part in the siege of Damascus, they clearly had an aggressive military role. New castles were built in strategic locations to guard the frontiers of the Crusader States, from the southern coastline near Ascalon, which was still in Egyptian hands until 1153, to the plain of Homs in Syria and the Taurus mountains in the north. Most of these castles were entrusted to the Templars and the Hospitallers. These include some of the most important building projects to have been undertaken in the two hundred years of the Crusader States' existence, such as the great Hospitaller castle of Krak des Chevaliers near Homs, and the Hospitaller castle of Margat in north Syria.

The Military Orders relied on Western support, both to gain manpower and to attract wealth. Despite the initial reservations of some churchmen, the idea of 'monastic knights' caught the imagination of twelfth-century Christendom. This was a way of perpetuating the ideals of the crusade, and by supporting the Military Orders one could at the same time contribute to the

Figure 3 Krak des Chevaliers, castle of the Hospitaller Knights near Homs, Syria. Built in the 1140s, the castle was extended to its present form in the thirteenth century and formed the centre of a large lordship. It surrendered to Baibars in 1270. (Source: Arian Zwegers, Flickr)

security of the Crusader States and ensure one's own salvation. Giving to the Military Orders, usually in the form of bequests from one's property after death, was seen in exactly the same terms as giving to monasteries. The Military Orders, though based for operational purposes in the East, had most of their property in the West, and this was used to finance their work in the Crusader States. A complex system of communication and financial and logistical support was needed to transfer men and materials of war from one end of Christendom to another. It is not surprising that both Military Orders developed early systems of credit and banking to facilitate these operations. For the individual recruit, becoming a Templar or Hospitaller was a way of combining a pious life of service without giving up one's military training. In a society in which most knights accepted that monastic life was a calling more likely than knighthood to merit an eternal reward, the assurance that these ways of life could be reconciled must have been a powerful attraction – less extreme than monasticism, but more meritorious than simply serving one's lord or fighting on behalf of one king against another.

By the 1140s, the kingdom of Jerusalem was secure: the threat from Egypt had receded, and Damascus was content to maintain a watchful neutrality. In north Syria, however, the Frankish settlers were under constant pressure from neighbouring Seljuq leaders. In 1119, the Franks in Antioch, led by Roger of Salerno, Tancred's brother-in-law and successor as ruler, were defeated in a catastrophic battle so devastating that it was known as the Field of Blood. Antioch never recovered its authority and, during the 1120s, had to be protected by the kingdom of Jerusalem. In the 1130s, King Fulk was less willing – and less able, because of his own domestic problems – to undertake this role, and Antioch came increasingly back into the orbit of the Byzantine Empire. The weakest of the Crusader States, however, was Edessa. Founded as an unintended consequence of Baldwin I's adventuring on the First Crusade, Edessa had the character of a frontier territory. Unlike Antioch, Jerusalem or the tiny principality of Tripoli squeezed between the two, Edessa never had the apparatus of a state. There were probably never more than a few hundred Frankish knights spread over an area of a few thousand square miles populated by a mixture of Armenians, Syrians, Arabs and Turks, most of whom – even the Christians among them – had little reason to love their new masters. To judge from the evidence of the chronicler Michael the Syrian, this was a lawless and dangerous society, and the Frankish counts had to be politically astute, bold and lucky to survive.

In 1144, Count Joscelin II made a fatal miscalculation when his boldness attracted the unfavourable attentions of a rising new Muslim power, Zengi, the ruler of Mosul. Although Zengi's ultimate strategic target was Damascus, he swept through Edessa and took the city amid scenes of slaughter on Christmas Eve 1144. Only the castles to the west of the Euphrates remained in Frankish hands. The news of this disaster, including the death of the Latin archbishop of Edessa during the sack of the city, reached the West in the form of a plea for military help from the ruler of Antioch, Raymond of Poitiers. Raymond, who had gone out to the East in similar circumstances to Fulk – to marry the heiress to the principality – feared that his territory would be attacked next. It was natural for Raymond to appeal for aid to the king of France, Louis VII, because Louis was married to Raymond's niece, Eleanor of Aquitaine.

But nothing happened until a year after Edessa had fallen, when Pope Eugenius III himself intervened. Eugenius' bull, directed specifically at the French nobility and knighthood, consciously sought to emulate Urban II's example of 1095. It was the first time that official recognition had been voiced that Urban's armed pilgrimage could be something more than a one-off event. Eugenius reminded the French knights of the heroic deeds of their grandfathers and urged them to take the cross in the same manner, to protect the Christians in the East. Although Eugenius spelled out the spiritual rewards of taking the cross more clearly than Urban had done, leaving little room for doubt that to crusade was to be saved, the response was muted at first. Few people in the West had heard of Edessa or cared much about its fate. As a cause, it could not compare with Jerusalem, which had already established a place in the minds of Christians as the iconic centre of their world. So when Eugenius, who had been a Cistercian monk before being elected pope, asked his former abbot Bernard of Clairvaux to preach the crusade, Bernard changed the spiritual direction of the crusade considerably. Almost all mention of Edessa or the geopolitical crisis presented by its capture was gone. Instead, Bernard appealed to the conscience of the knights and to their fears for their own salvation. God had allowed Edessa to fall, he argued, so that Christian knights could show their devotion to God – by taking the cross – and thus earn salvation. The fact that the original conception of crusading was an armed pilgrimage to Jerusalem was glossed over because Jerusalem was not in any danger. Bernard therefore concentrated on the interior spirituality of the crusader rather than on the crusade's real purpose in the East.

Bernard's preaching was so compelling that over the course of 1146 many of the French nobility took the cross. Louis VII had already announced his intention to make an armed pilgrimage to Jerusalem – in other words, to lead an army east to support the kingdom's military endeavours – but until Bernard's intervention he had not received much support. During 1146, a major expedition was planned, enlarged by the unexpected addition of Emperor Conrad III with a German army. Bernard's recruiting activities may, indeed, have taken matters further than Eugenius had intended. A group of Saxon knights petitioned the papacy, through the offices of Bernard, for permission to take a crusading vow not for an expedition to the East but one against the pagan inhabitants of Pomerania, on what is now the Baltic coast of eastern Germany and Poland. This campaign, from 1147 to 1149, marked the beginning of the Baltic crusades, which were to continue well into the fourteenth century. It also formalized the extension of crusading – holy war for the specific spiritual benefit of penance – to a non-Muslim enemy.

At the same time, Bernard's preaching helped recruitment for another expedition timed to coincide with the crusade to the East. Afonso Enriquez I of Portugal – a new kingdom created from the expansionist militarism of the kingdom of Castile in the late eleventh and early twelfth century – was attempting to conquer Lisbon, which was in Muslim hands. For this an amphibious expedition was required, so that the city could be encircled by land and cut off from supplies by sea. A fleet was recruited from southern English, Norman and Flemish knights and sailors, the intention being that this force could sail to Portugal from the

English Channel, assist in the siege of Lisbon and make its way through the Straits of Gibraltar and east through the Mediterranean to Syria. The plan worked in part: the fleet did indeed take part in the successful conquest of Porto, but it then dispersed in a series of further raids along the coast and never reached the East. Nevertheless, the chronicler who reported the events, an eyewitness named Raoul, was in no doubt that the Lisbon expedition was in every sense a holy war. At the same time, a Genoese force took part in the Catalan conquest of Tortosa, on the Mediterranean coast of Catalonia, from the Arabs. Crusading in the 1140s crisscrossed the Christian world.

The Second Crusade in the East had all the advantages that the First had lacked: knowledge of conditions, royal organization and financing, and a Frankish population in the East eagerly awaiting its assistance. Yet the crusaders and the eastern Franks between them squandered all these advantages and the campaign ended in failure. Perhaps the only disadvantage compared to the First Crusade was the lack of Byzantine support, and it was this that proved crucial to the outcome. The French and German armies failed to co-ordinate their activities in Asia Minor, and Conrad set off across the Bosphorus in advance of Louis. Without Byzantine help, Conrad, who had divided his army into two, was defeated heavily by the Seljuqs at Dorylaeum in October 1147 and returned to Constantinople with his forces much reduced. Louis, after a bad-tempered stay in Constantinople as guest of the reluctant emperor Manuel Komnenos, took the route around the western coast of Asia Minor, but in January 1148 his army, too, fell prey to the Seljuqs, and he abandoned the march across Asia Minor, setting sail with his tattered forces for Antioch from Adalia on the south coast. Louis and the French blamed Manuel for his refusal to support them, but the Byzantine situation was very different from that in 1095. Manuel had recently negotiated a treaty with the Seljuq sultan of Asia Minor, Mesud I, and had no wish to antagonize him into a war for which he was not prepared. The politics of the Crusader States also complicated matters considerably. Louis knew very well that the main Byzantine ambition in the East was to exercise the overlordship of Antioch that they considered they had been cheated out of by Bohemond in 1098. During the 1130s, Manuel's father John had come close to securing this by military intervention, but Antioch was too far away to be controlled from a distance. Antioch's position was greatly weakened by the fall of Edessa to Zengi, but from a Byzantine perspective a Western army campaigning in north Syria might only strengthen it again. Yet John had proposed that if Raymond of Antioch could take Aleppo, he should restore Antioch to the Byzantine Empire, and this could only happen with external aid. For this reason, Manuel was ambivalent about the whole enterprise.

Louis VII realized that he was also trapped by political circumstance. The original plan had been for the crusade to recover Edessa, but this was no longer realistic. In 1146, Joscelin II had tried to retake his lost city but, when he failed, Nur ad-Din destroyed the city altogether. There was nothing for the crusade to recover: Frankish territory east of the Euphrates was gone forever. Zengi had been murdered in September 1146, but an assault on Aleppo, to relieve pressure on Antioch and reduce the power of Zengi's successor, Nur ad-Din, now made the most strategic sense. It was certainly what Raymond wanted, but perhaps he pressed too hard for it. Naturally he did so by appealing to Louis through his niece Eleanor, who had accompanied Louis on the crusade. This was later misconstrued by the historian of the kingdom of Jerusalem, William of Tyre, as an affair between Eleanor and Raymond, which led to the furious withdrawal of his army from Antioch by Louis VII in summer 1148. But it was in any case a reduced army, and Louis may have judged that in order to accomplish anything he would need the support of the kingdom of Jerusalem as well as of Antioch. Besides, the crusader conquest of Aleppo would lead to renewed Byzantine demands over Antioch. Louis took his forces to Acre, where at a council in June 1148 it was decided to mount a joint attack – with King Baldwin III of Jerusalem – against Damascus.

This fateful decision has continued to puzzle historians. Damascus had never posed a threat to the kingdom of Jerusalem – in fact, the Damascenes wanted nothing so much as to preserve their independence from the Zengids in north Syria. On the other hand, Damascus had been a target of the kingdom as early as 1127, and the policy of a pre-emptive strike before Nur ad-Din's influence could spread too far to the south may have been far-sighted. Besides, Baldwin, who had been crowned king as an infant alongside his mother, Melisende, and father, Fulk, in 1131, was now a young man of eighteen who wanted to prove himself. Fulk had died in 1143, but Melisende showed no sign of relinquishing power. Extending the kingdom's territory by annexing the rich and historic city of Damascus would help Baldwin to assert his own authority.

The siege was a damp squib. In the course of five days in late July 1148, the crusade fizzled out in scenes of indecisiveness and mutual recriminations. Conrad had not thought much of the idea in the first place, preferring an attack on Egyptian-held Ascalon, but he was overruled. The crusaders took up position in the orchards to the west of the city, but the terrain, with low mud walls and squat towers enclosing individual plots, made it easy for marauding parties from the city to hinder their progress, and once they were within sight of the city walls, they moved to the south-east, where the defences were considered to be weaker. In hindsight this proved a disastrous decision. They were unable to make any headway in besieging the city, and suspicions began to develop amongst them about each others' real intentions. Baldwin and his barons suspected that a deal had been done to give the city to a Western crusader, Thierry, count of Flanders. The Western sources blame the local baronage for deliberately undermining the siege by moving the army to a less favourable location. By the time the news spread that Nur ad-Din was on the march with an army to dislodge them, the crusaders had had enough, and a fierce sortie on 25 July was enough to persuade them to withdraw. Nothing further was achieved, and after completing their pilgrimage vows to Jerusalem, the crusaders returned home in disappointment.

A year later, Raymond of Antioch was defeated and killed in battle by Nur's forces, and the project of conquering Aleppo looked further away than ever. In 1154, Nur ad-Din walked into Damascus unopposed. Given the crusaders' assault in 1148, the Damascenes could no longer rely on neutrality to protect them. Looking back at the events of 1147–8, William of Tyre wrote that it was from this time that the decline of the kingdom's fortunes could be dated. Even allowing for the gift of hindsight, it was a perceptive assessment. Perhaps most important was the realization that the interests of crusaders from the West and the settlers in the East did not invariably coincide. Much as the Crusader States needed Western help, the price was sometimes too high.

The 1150s and 1160s saw the kingdom of Jerusalem at its height. Ascalon was captured in 1153, and the demise of the Egyptians was sealed by the invasion of Egypt by King Amalric I in 1167 and 1169. But although this may have seemed impressive, it upset the precarious balance of power in the East. In response to Amalric's invasion, Nur ad-Din sent an army to Egypt to prevent it coming into the orbit of the kingdom of Jerusalem. Egypt fell into Nur's hands in 1169 when his general Shirkuh drove off the Frankish army. By 1171, the Fatimid caliphate of Egypt had been suppressed with the death of the last caliph, and power in Egypt now lay with Nur's general there – Shirkuh's nephew Saladin.

There was probably little to worry the Franks before the fateful year of 1174. In the space of a few months, both Nur and King Amalric died. Both left young boys as heirs, and both successions, in Damascus and Jerusalem, were troubled. We will examine Saladin's rise to power as a result of this in a separate chapter. The heir to the kingdom of Jerusalem was the thirteen-year-old son of Amalric, Baldwin IV. We know a good deal about both Amalric and Baldwin because William of Tyre served as the young heir's tutor, and it was he who discovered the terrible truth about the boy when he was only about seven years old. Watching him play-fighting with friends, William noticed that Baldwin never seemed to feel hurt by any of the bruises and scrapes he suffered. His nerve endings were already defective – the boy had leprosy. The disease progresses very slowly in the young, and the diagnosis was not yet certain when he was crowned in 1174. In any case, there was no real alternative. His sister, Sibylla, was younger than he, and the closest male relatives on both his father Amalric's and his mother Agnes of Courtenay's side had been captured in battle in 1164 and were still prisoners. By 1176, however, both had returned from captivity. Now there were, if anything, too many powerful barons willing to advise and direct affairs.

The closest relative on his father's side of the family was Raymond III, count of Tripoli, whose father, Raymond II, had married a daughter of King Baldwin II of Jerusalem. Raymond III himself married Eschiva, the widowed heiress of the fief of Tiberias, giving him a powerful hold on the kingdom of Jerusalem as well as the nominally autonomous – but in fact militarily weak – county of Tripoli. When Raymond, already an experienced soldier and politician, demanded the regency of the kingdom of Jerusalem, he met little resistance; in fact, he was supported by much of the baronage of the kingdom. The closest eligible relative on Baldwin's mother's side was Joscelin III of Courtenay, the brother of Baldwin's mother, Agnes. The Courtenays were a First-Crusade family who had ruled Edessa from 1118 to 1146 before withdrawing to the kingdom of Jerusalem. As the king's uncle, Joscelin had a closer familial tie to Baldwin, though not a better claim of his own to the throne, than Raymond. Amalric, who was Baldwin III's younger brother, had divorced Agnes when he unexpectedly became king in 1164 in order to marry, for reasons of state, a Byzantine princess, Maria Komnena. From this marriage a daughter, Isabella, was born. The children of the king thus comprised a leper and two girls. Because of his illness, Baldwin could not father children, so the kingdom's future would depend on the marriage of the next in line, Sibylla.

Raymond, as regent, devoted much of his period in office to resolving the question of succession. The traditional policy was to seek husbands for heiresses in the West. Here the kingdom was simply unlucky. In 1176, Sibylla married William Longsword, the heir to the marquisate of Montferrat in the Savoy. Montferrat was not only resource-rich but also a fief of the Holy Roman Empire, which meant that William, as king of Jerusalem by marriage, could have expected to count on the support of the most powerful ruler in the West. But two years later this rosy picture had changed. Soon after fathering a child, Baldwin V, William died – apparently of food poisoning after ill-advisedly eating seafood on a hot day. Another possible husband, the duke of Burgundy, declined the offer of marriage. Meanwhile, Baldwin's condition grew steadily worse. Despite this, in 1177 he won a victory in battle over Saladin near Gaza that was all the more impressive because he no longer had the use of his right arm and therefore had to control his horse with his knees in order to leave one arm free to hold a sword. One reason why the victory was so unexpected was that it was fought with a tiny army, because the regent and most of the kingdom's barons had rejected royal policy in order to campaign fruitlessly in the north.

By 1180, Baldwin was so worried about Raymond's conduct of policy that he allowed Sibylla to marry a recent immigrant from France who must have seemed several degrees below her first husband in status. Guy of Lusignan had little to recommend him apart from a reputation for chivalric conduct, but he was unproven as a war leader and a politician and was to prove inept at both. In fact, Baldwin had little choice. There were signs that Raymond might seize the throne for himself, suppressing the succession of Sibylla's young son. The presence of this child was some reassurance of the future succession, but in one way he also hampered his mother's chances of finding the kind of husband in the West who might prove genuinely useful, for no high-profile figure was likely to accept being regent for his predecessor's heir. As Sibylla's husband, Guy took over the duties of regent from Raymond. But he did not have the confidence of all the barons, and in 1183, when Saladin invaded Galilee, he did not trust his army to battle and simply waited for Saladin to withdraw without being tempted into a confrontation. Baldwin IV, furious at what he saw as a missed opportunity, disgraced Guy and crowned Baldwin V, now seven years old, as co-ruler, with Raymond and the boy's

Figure 4 This image illustrates William of Tyre's account of how he realized that the young Baldwin IV had leprosy. (Source: From a thirteenth-century French manuscript of the *Histoire d'Outremer*, comprising William of Tyre's *Chronicle* with continuations up to 1332, British Library Yates Thompson MS 12, f. 152v.)

uncle Joscelin as regent and guardian, respectively. Further tragedy struck. Baldwin IV's death in 1185 was not unexpected, but he was followed to the grave only a year later by his unfortunate nephew, whose health had never been robust.

Baldwin IV had proposed that, in this eventuality, the succession should be determined between Sibylla (and thus Guy) and her half-sister Isabella, who was married to a baron of the kingdom, Humphrey of Toron. This was, of course, a snub to Guy, whose competence to rule Baldwin doubted. But the international committee of the great and the good whom Baldwin had envisaged deliberating over the problem – the pope, Holy Roman Emperor and kings of England and France – never had the chance to determine the succession, because Sibylla and Guy acted. With the support of the patriarch of Jerusalem, the Templars and one of the kingdom's most powerful barons, the pugnacious Reynald of Châtillon, they staged a coup and had themselves crowned. Raymond went into internal exile without acknowledging Guy as king, and the baronage was divided. Such divisive politics were possible only because a truce with Saladin had been in operation since before Baldwin IV's death. But Reynald impetuously broke this early in 1187 when, from his fief of Transjordan, which stood guard over the desert road from Damascus to the Red Sea, he attacked a caravan of Muslim pilgrims to Mecca. Among the pilgrims was Saladin's own sister. Not surprisingly, Saladin had public opinion among the influential in the Islamic world on his side, and the army that he gathered to invade the kingdom in the summer of 1187 was the largest that had been amassed since the First Crusade.

The kingdom of Jerusalem was well prepared to meet the invasion. A substantial number of knights had come from England and France to help the kingdom in its hour of need, paid for by a fund made available by Henry II of England in expiation of the murder of Archbishop Thomas Becket seventeen years earlier. The kingdom's castles and fortified towns were left with only skeleton garrisons so as to make as large a field army as possible available to Guy. He probably led a force of over a thousand knights, with about ten times as many infantry. It would have been more had many Templars not been killed in a foolish skirmish with Saladin's reconnaissance force in the spring.

Saladin began offensive operations in June by besieging Tiberias, the main stronghold in Raymond of Tripoli's fief in Galilee. It was a clever move. At the last minute, faced with invasion, Raymond had agreed to fight with Guy. Attacking Tiberias might be a means of dislodging that reluctant support. But although his wife and stepsons were holed up there, Raymond advised caution. The Franks should wait for Saladin to overextend and commit himself, rather than marching impetuously to the relief of Tiberias. Guy summoned the kingdom's army to Sephoria, a castle near Nazareth, about fifteen miles away across the Galilee plain. One of the entourage of the Ibelins, a noble family who supported Raymond, has left a vivid account of the series of events that led to the disastrous Battle of Hattin on 4 July. In council, Raymond's advice prevailed, but Reynald and the Grand Master of the Templars, Gerard of Rideford, badgered the king to attack Saladin. Guy was persuaded and led the army to its doom. Although the distance was not great, the route lay across a waterless plain, and the army had to march in full armour at the height of summer. They were watched and sniped at all the way by Saladin's outriders, until at last, in a futile search for a spring, they halted for the night at the shallow hill of Hattin, almost within sight of Tiberias. Here, in the early morning of 4 July, Saladin was able to surround and squeeze the Frankish army. Guy had systematically flouted all the rules governing combat with the Turks, and the kingdom of Jerusalem paid for his mistakes. Even so, the battle was not won until late in the day. Raymond and a party of his knights broke through the Muslim ranks but fled the battlefield. Most of the rest were unable to charge and were overcome by weight of numbers in a series of dense melees.

THE BATTLE OF HATTIN

Saladin invaded the kingdom of Jerusalem in spring 1187 with about 30,000 troops and at the end of June embarked on the siege of Tiberias, on the west coast of the Sea of Galilee. In response, King Guy of Jerusalem mustered about 1,200 knights and as many as 18,000 foot soldiers at Sephoria, near Nazareth. The advice from his barons and the Military Orders was far from unanimous, but on the evening of 2 July, Guy was swayed by the insistence of Reynald of Châtillon and the Templar Grand Master, Gerard of Ridefort, to leave the safety of his defensive position and march to the relief of Tiberias. Saladin had already moved the bulk of his army to the plateau at Kufr Sabt, only ten miles from Sephoria, in an attempt to lure Guy away. The march to Tiberias across the parched Galilee landscape was difficult because, in an attempt to cover the ground quickly and gain some element of surprise, the Christians had not taken supplies of water for either men or horses. Tactically this proved disastrous because the direction of the march came to be determined by the possible availability of water at springs on the way to Tiberias. They stopped halfway at Maskana, about three miles from the springs at the village of Hattin. The rearguard of the Christian army had come under constant attack already, and on the night of 3 July, Saladin's main army came up to within about a mile of the Christian camp. The next day, the Christians organized themselves into battle order, trying to co-ordinate the mounted knights with the foot soldiers. No exact account of the battle survives, but it seems likely that Saladin was able to prevent this from happening with the result that the infantry fled up the hill to the north, the Horns of Hattin. Raymond of Tripoli charged his squadron at the Muslims, but they did little damage because the Muslims parted their line to allow the charge to dissipate. Eventually the Christian army found itself encircled on the Horns of Hattin, where they fought a rearguard action that lasted much of the day, until they were overwhelmed and the leaders, including Guy, Reynald and Gerard of Ridefort, were captured.

Hundreds of Frankish knights were taken prisoner, and the True Cross, the precious relic that was carried into battle by every king of Jerusalem, was lost forever.

After the battle, Guy found himself a prisoner alongside Reynald of Châtillon in Saladin's tent. Guy was treated well and led off to an honourable captivity, but not before he had to watch as Reynald was executed, perhaps by Saladin's own hand. All the Templar and Hospitaller Knights who had been taken prisoner in the battle were executed at Saladin's orders – a backhanded compliment to their effectiveness. The battle had been so decisive that Saladin was easily able to overrun the kingdom. Most of the major towns, with the sole exception of Tyre, fell to him over the next year. Most important symbolically was Jerusalem. Although stoutly defended by Balian of Ibelin, it could not resist a long siege and fell to Saladin in early October 1187. Saladin's merciful treatment of both civilians and armed defenders, many of whom were allowed to leave freely on payment of a ransom, could not erase the sense of disaster, signalled by the loss of the holy city. The news of Hattin and the subsequent fall of Jerusalem shocked the West profoundly. After three generations, the assumption of Christian control of Jerusalem had become second nature. Now Christendom had to get used once again to sentiments that had lain dormant since 1099.

5

The Islamic reaction: Zengi, Nur ad-Din and Saladin

On the eve of the First Crusade, the Islamic world in the Near East was divided in just about every way imaginable: not only politically but also along religious and cultural fault lines. The Seljuqs, who had taken over political leadership of the region from the Abbasids during the eleventh century, had managed to maintain single unified rule for a couple of generations, but this came to an end in 1092 with the death of the powerful Malik Shah. Although they had conquered Asia Minor from the Byzantine Empire in the 1070s, they had never extended their power to Egypt, which had been under the control of the Shi'ite Fatimid dynasty since 969. The Holy Land was a front line between Fatimids and Seljuqs, and in 1098, during the First Crusade, the Fatimids recaptured it. Elsewhere, Seljuq control was patchy, even before Malik Shah's death. Antioch, for example, remained in Byzantine hands until 1086, and throughout Syria, from the valleys of the Upper Euphrates and Tigris to the coastal ports, independent Armenian and Arab rulers maintained precarious authority over their own territories as long as they recognized Seljuq overlordship. The Seljuqs, a Turkic people originally from central Asia, were probably not all that numerous and remained a minority elite ruling over largely Arabic-speaking populations. The Arab populations themselves were divided on religious grounds: many, especially in the Holy Land, were Greek Orthodox Christians, while some areas of northern Syria were also Christian but followed the Syriac Orthodox Church. Large groups of Armenians, who were also Christian, had settled in south-east Asia Minor and in the Upper Euphrates basin in the eleventh century.

These structural splits within the regions under Seljuq rule were exacerbated by succession disputes following Malik Shah's death. Asia Minor was contested between two rival families, while in Syria the major centres of population – Damascus, Aleppo and Mosul – were controlled by different claimants to Malik Shah's empire. These splits undoubtedly made the task of the first crusaders easier, because it meant they could confront individual rulers rather than unified forces. Even when the Seljuqs did succeed in mounting unified opposition, for example when Duqaq, emir of Damascus, sent an army to join his brother Ridwan of Aleppo's forces in the battle for Antioch, it proved a short-term and ineffective measure.

None of the Islamic leaders treated the crusade as anything other than a traditional war for territory. Nor was there any reason why they should not have done so. Most contemporary Arab writers assumed that the Franks were mercenary forces fighting to extend Byzantine territory. After all, Normans had been serving in this capacity alongside English, Scandinavians and other non-Greeks for some time before the 1090s. Even in the early thirteenth century, when crusading had long been understood in the Islamic world as religiously motivated, the Arab writer Ibn al-Athir interpreted the cause of the First Crusade as economic rather than spiritual. A measure of Muslim failure to understand crusading in its own terms can be seen in 1105, when an imam in Damascus, as-Sulami, tried to preach resistance against the Franks as a jihad – he was largely ignored. Naturally, both Seljuq and Fatimid rulers tried to dislodge the Frankish settlers from the new lands they had made their own. In so doing, they treated the Franks simply as another rival grouping on a complex political map.

Thus they were quite prepared to make treaties with the Crusader States. Sometimes, as in the war between Antioch and Edessa in 1105, rival Seljuq leaders were prepared to ally with rival Franks.

It took a long time for this attitude to change; in fact, one could say that it remained a constant underlying factor in Muslim dealings with the Franks throughout the period of crusader settlement in the East. By the 1180s, however, a new element had entered the relationship between the Islamic world and the Frankish settlers, and the war of conquest launched by Saladin against the kingdom of Jerusalem was, as far as he was concerned, a holy war. How did this shift in attitude come about?

The first real signs of change appeared in 1119. Il-Ghazi's spectacular victory over the Franks of Antioch at the Field of Blood made a big impression in the Seljuq world and was celebrated in verse and tomb inscriptions in terms that suggest it was regarded as a triumph of Islamic forces over Christian. Similarly, the inscription on the tomb of Balaq marks his defeat and capture of Baldwin II in religious terms. The picture is much clearer twenty or so years later, when Edessa fell to Zengi. By the 1140s the ideal of jihad was being revived throughout the Islamic world. It had long been dormant in Syria, but Zengi, though he rose to power as ruler of Mosul, had been brought up in Iraq, where religious and legal scholarship had never lost sight of the ideal. In the far west of the Islamic world, too, revivalism was in the air. The rise of the Almohad dynasty in Morocco and their invasion of Spain breathed new life into resistance to the Christian reconquest of the Iberian peninsula at the same time as Zengi was flexing his muscles in north Syria. Even though Zengi had probably not been intending to conquer Edessa, he was astute enough to realize that he could use the unexpected victory to boost his standing with the caliphate and the religious authorities in the Islamic world.

Although Zengi was respected by Seljuq and Arab contemporaries for his military prowess, he was not widely loved. In fact, stories told about him by Arab writers emphasize his cruelty and harshness even to his own subjects and allies. He ruled through fear. One story has him giving the order to soldiers marching through cornfields that any who strayed off the path and trampled the corn would be crucified. The manner of his death – he was assassinated by a slave driven to desperation by his cruel treatment – testifies to the way he was regarded among his own people. The benefits of Zengi's rule for the cause of Islamic resistance to the Franks would be seen only in the generations after his death. Zengi's most lasting achievement was not the conquest of Edessa, but the establishment of madrasas throughout the areas under his control. Religious colleges attached to mosques dedicated to the instruction of young men in Islamic law and theology were widespread in Iraq, but not in the relative backwaters of Syria and Palestine. Similarly, he established kanqahs, religious communities that have been compared to Christian monasteries, to promote a religious revival among Muslims in north Syria. The real significance of these foundations is that legal, theological and spiritual education was in the hands of the Arabic-speaking intellectuals, who had been all but ignored by previous Seljuq rulers. The introduction of madrasas, where the offspring of the Seljuq ruling military caste could be educated, would produce a generation of rulers who were imbued with the religious values that had often seemed to be lacking in their predecessors. This alliance of power and faith did more to integrate Seljuqs and Arabs than anything previously accomplished.

Nowhere was this new balance of power more evident than in Damascus. This city, one of the major centres of population and culture in Syria, had since *c.*1112 maintained a sometimes uneasy neutrality in the face of the growth of the kingdom of Jerusalem. Damascus, though controlled until 1128 by the Seljuq Tughtegin, had a large and powerful Shi'ite presence. The Seljuqs, who were staunch Sunnis, regarded the Shi'ites as heretics, hardly better than Franks, but Tughtegin's son Buri was unproven, and since the vizier al-Mazdaghani was himself a Shi'ite, it must have looked like a perfect opportunity for the Shi'ite community to take over the city. But Buri was not to be so easily dominated, and after a council meeting in the palace he had the vizier openly murdered. The riots that followed, in which hundreds of Shi'ite families were massacred, demonstrated the full extent of Sunni resentment against the hold they felt the vizier exercised over the city. Ibn al-Athir, who was himself a Sunni, later rationalized the outbreak of violence by suggesting that al-Mazdaghani had made a secret deal with Baldwin II of Jerusalem to hand over Damascus to him in return for Tyre. This is unlikely, given the huge efforts that the kingdom of Jerusalem had made to capture Tyre in 1123–4 – in fact, they had been unable to do so without substantial help from Venice, and the Venetians were unlikely to give up the concessions they had gained as a result. Yet it must have seemed plausible to Damascene Sunnis at the time, because a Frankish attack on Damascus was feared, and the fact that Shi'ite refugees from the massacre were welcomed by Baldwin II added credence.

In the event, Damascus held out easily enough against Baldwin's attempted conquest of 1129, but Buri could not escape the vengeance of the Shi'ites. An assassination attempt was made against him in 1131, and he died a year later of his wounds. His son, Ismail, was unable to break free of the cycle of suspicion, plots and violence that took hold of Damascus throughout the 1130s. Caught between fear of assassination at the hands of the Shi'ites at home and of Zengi's growing power in the north, Ismail tried to tread a path between the two, using the kingdom of Jerusalem as a counterweight. It worked only until 1135, when Ismail was also murdered. Zengi was actually on the point of marching to take over Damascus when he learned that one of Tughtegin's emirs, Mu'in ad-Din Unur, had seized control himself. For the next fifteen years, Unur more or less succeeded in holding Damascus on its own course of watchful neutrality between Zengi in the north and the Franks to the south. The kingdom of Jerusalem came to regard Damascus as a neutral buffer zone between itself and the theatres of war to the north, and this policy was underlined by a treaty between King Fulk and Unur in 1140, the intention of which was to protect Damascus against Zengi's ambitions. Although there were episodes that threatened to undermine

USAMAH IBN MUNQIDH (1095–1188)

Usamah was born into the ruling dynasty of the small autonomous state of Shaizar, which occupied a precarious but strategically important position between Antioch and Aleppo. He went into exile in 1137 for fear of arousing the jealousy of its ruler, his uncle. He initially entered the service of Zengi, but by 1138 he was a follower of Unur, the governor of Damascus, on whose behalf he undertook diplomatic missions to Jerusalem between 1138 and 1143. In 1144, he fled to Cairo when he fell under suspicion of trying to overthrow Unur, and offered his services to the Fatimid regime. After 1154 he fled Cairo for the same reason, this time being suspected of conspiring against the Fatimid ruler, and returned to Damascus, where Nur ad-Din had assumed control. He fought with Nur against Jerusalem in 1162 and 1164, before taking service with the Artuqid emir Kara Arslan in north Syria. In 1174 he returned to Damascus and became a prominent adviser of Saladin. Usamah is known as the author of a number of works, the most famous of which is the *Kitab al-I'tibar,* or *Book of Contemplation*. Because he recounts in this book episodes from his varied experience of Seljuq, Fatimid and Frankish political society, it is sometimes regarded as a memoir, though in fact its purpose was moral instruction. Nevertheless, it remains one of the most colourful and informative sources not only for our knowledge of the politics of the Islamic world of the twelfth century, but of how a cultivated and well-connected Arab Muslim regarded his contemporaries. It is particularly valuable for providing insightful, though not necessarily typical, views of the Franks.

this balance of power, little had happened to upset it before the Second Crusade so unexpectedly launched its forces against the city in the summer of 1148.

By this time, a new hero had begun to emerge in the Islamic world. Zengi, at the moment of his triumph with the final destruction of Frankish rule in Edessa in 1146, suffered the fate of so many Seljuq leaders when he was murdered. His second son, Nur ad-Din, immediately took over the reins of power in Aleppo. Nur was already a mature man of twenty-nine, with a style of authority quite different from that of his father. Where Zengi had been prone to fits of anger and violence, Nur maintained an outward show of calmness combined with inner strength. He had already cultivated a reputation for deep piety, and he came to be seen as a ruler who ruled to maintain Islamic ideals rather than, as his father had, because he enjoyed power for its own sake. For all his religious sincerity, however, Nur was no less ruthless than Zengi. In fact, he was rigid in his pursuit of Sunni orthodoxy, and his justice, though rooted in legal tradition rather than in service of his own aims, was no less demanding.

The Frankish failure at Damascus was a lucky break for Nur. Unur's death from dysentery a year after beating off the crusaders left Damascus in the hands of a sixteen-year-old descendant of Tughtegin, while at the same time Nur took advantage of the crusade's failure to intervene in north Syria to attack Antioch. At the Battle of Inab in June 1149, his armies won a resounding victory in which Prince Raymond was killed, apparently by a Kurdish commander of Nur's called Shirkuh. This man and his family would prove to loom large in the history of Islamic resistance to the crusaders. The defeat of Antioch left the way clear for Nur to turn his attention to Damascus, the prize that had eluded Zengi. The letter he wrote to the Damascenes was couched in the language of protection and friendship: his offer to help the city against future Frankish attack was no more than a sacred duty enjoined on him as a good Muslim. It was a none

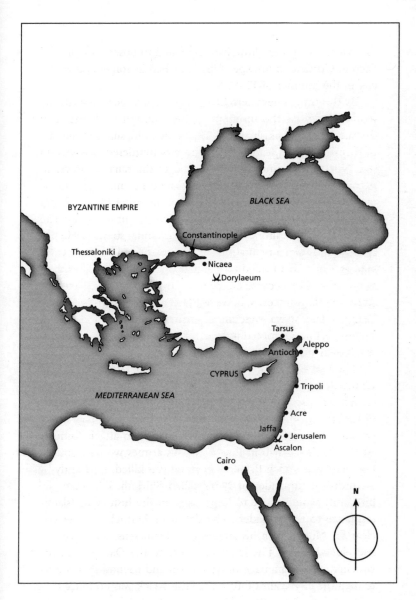

Map 2: The Eastern Mediterranean

too subtle attempt to undermine Damascene confidence in the
capacity of their own leader, 'Abaq, to defend them against the
Franks, but in the long run it worked. Although the kingdom of
Jerusalem had swiftly restored the 1140 treaty with Damascus
after the failure of the Second Crusade, Nur had succeeded in
reminding the Damascenes that there was a Muslim alternative
and one that had their best interests at heart. Nur's name began to
appear in the Friday sermons at the Great Mosque. The campaign
of persuasion continued, and in 1150 he wrote to the Damascenes
again, this time mentioning the virtues of jihad against the Franks.
Over the next few years, he succeeded by these tactics of appealing to a sense of Islamic unity in loosening the allegiance of the
Damascenes to 'Abaq. His own position weakened, 'Abaq could
only look to the alliance with King Fulk for support, which of
course only aggravated the situation. By spring 1154, 'Abaq could
no longer count on his own militia and Nur struck. By intercept-
ing convoys of food from other parts of Syria to Damascus, he
first pushed up the price of bread so as to foment dissatisfaction
with 'Abaq; then, when he appeared with an army in person, the
citizens opened the gates to him. He had won Damascus, the
greatest prize in Syria, without having to strike a blow in anger
against fellow Muslims. Ibn al-Qalanisi, the Damascene chronicler
who had seen and reported everything that had happened to the
city since the First Crusade, wrote that when Nur appeared the
whole population turned out to applaud him and offer prayers
for his long life. The significance of Nur's triumph was that, for
the first time since before 1092, the main centres of population,
wealth and power in Syria, Aleppo and Damascus were in the
hands of a single ruler.

Nur's intentions as ruler of Syria were open from the start.
They were signalled in two highly symbolic acts. One was the
rebuilding of the law court in Damascus, which announced Nur's
devotion not only to Islamic law as a concept but to his own role
as law-giver and maintainer of the laws. His was to be no arbitrary

rulership, but one founded on principles of justice in accordance with the faithful interpretation of Sunni legal orthodoxy. The second act was the commission of a new *minbar* for the Great Mosque in Damascus. The *minbar,* or pulpit, from which the Friday sermon was preached, was a standard feature of mosques. The symbolism was twofold. Nur was signalling his reliance on religious teachers to undertake the spread of his message: the extension of Sunni orthodoxy to the whole *umma,* the world of the faithful. The alliance between scholarship, faith and power envisaged by Zengi was established in Damascus. But equally important was the reason Nur gave for the construction of the new *minbar*. For this was not to stay in the Great Mosque in Damascus – prestigious though that was. Its ultimate destination was a spiritually more important mosque – the Al-Aqsa mosque in Jerusalem.

The Al-Aqsa, or 'far-off' mosque, was considered the third-holiest site in the Islamic world, after the mosques in Mecca and Medina, the places of the Prophet's birth and death. The special importance of Jerusalem for Muslims derived from the celebrated 'night journey' of the prophet, in which an angel guided his horse from Medina to Jerusalem in a single night. But despite being firmly established in Islamic religious tradition, and although it had been in Muslim hands since 638, Jerusalem had never yet gained the place that many pious Muslims thought it deserved in the *umma*. It had a thriving legal school, and pilgrims from across the Islamic world visited it, and yet Jerusalem remained something of a backwater. Moreover, the only attempts by Muslims to recapture it in the half-century since its fall to the crusaders in 1099 had been undertaken by the Fatimid regime in Egypt – and even these had fizzled out within twenty years of the First Crusade. When Nur took control there, no ruler of Damascus had seriously targeted Jerusalem for forty years, and, significantly, none of the jihad discourses promoted by or on behalf of Seljuq rulers linked Jerusalem with the holy war. It was Nur ad-Din who began the process that was to culminate in 1187, of making recovery of Jerusalem the explicit aim of the jihad. The process took the form, typical of Nur's approach, of inculcating ideas in the minds of Muslims. It is from Nur's reign that we see a new literary form, the 'praises of Jerusalem', in verse or prose form, to be read and listened to in mosques and madrasas. It was all part of what has been called 'the jihad of the tongue': Nur's attempt to enthuse the Islamic world with jihad ideals. Of course, such methods were only effective because they were confirmed by Nur's own character. Unlike many previous Seljuq rulers, Nur seemed genuinely to live by his religious ideals. His personal piety was beyond doubt, but he was also austere, sober and quiet in his private life, and he encouraged the same in his officers. There were no luxurious feasts or musical parties in Aleppo or Damascus under his rule.

Despite the attention he focused on Jerusalem as the ultimate destination of the jihad, Nur did not directly attack the Frankish kingdom. He sought instead to weaken the Franks whenever possible and to benefit gradually from incremental advances. Thus, in 1164 he attacked the Principality of Antioch, scoring a notable victory in a battle at Artah, in Syria, in which the count of Tripoli and prince of Antioch were captured. But in fact this was a diversionary feint designed to draw attention away from his real strategy, which concerned a fast-developing political situation far to the south, in Egypt. For a long time real power in Egypt had rested not with the Fatimid caliphs but with their viziers, but the position was one surrounded by danger. In 1162 a new vizier, Shawar, came to power, but was soon ousted by a rival, Dirgham. Shawar took refuge with Nur ad-Din, and Nur was persuaded to help restore him to power in Cairo. There was good sense behind this policy, because the new king of Jerusalem, Amalric, had also begun to turn his attention to the easy pickings he thought could be gained along the Nile. Although the once fearsome military and naval might of the Fatimids had waned, Egypt was still wealthy and civilized. Valuable products – silks, spices, gold – flowed into

Egypt from Saharan Africa and the Indian Ocean trade. Amalric had inherited an annual tribute payable to the crown of Jerusalem for not intervening in Egypt, but he must have reasoned that the conquest of the caliphate would yield far more. Nur watched Amalric's first invasion of Egypt in 1162 from the sidelines, but although the Franks got no further than an abortive siege of the town of Bilbais, on an eastern branch of the Nile, this was close enough to Cairo to worry Nur. In 1164, rather than allow the kingdom of Jerusalem to grow any more powerful, he sent an army under the Kurd Shirkuh to restore Shawar to power. Once in power, however, Shawar reneged on his promises to Nur and invited Amalric back to Egypt to help him drive the Seljuqs out. Amalric, of course, was only too pleased to respond, and it was in order to relieve the pressure on Shirkuh, besieged in Bilbais, that Nur launched his attack on Harim. The capture of Raymond III of Tripoli and Bohemond III of Antioch was enough of a crisis for the Crusader States to persuade Amalric to abandon the invasion of Egypt and return home.

In 1167, Amalric, once again with Shawar's support, tried again, but Shirkuh held off the Franks in a pitched battle and then seized Alexandria, far to the north and west at the other end of the Nile Delta, to draw the Franks away from Cairo. Amalric refused to abandon the war, though by now it was proving hugely expensive – it all but ruined the Hospitallers. Finally, in 1169, the Fatimid caliph, the adolescent al-'Adid, himself intervened to break the stranglehold that the alliance between his vizier and the Franks exercised over Egypt, and Shirkuh, with his nephew Saladin, finally drove Amalric's forces out of the country. The winner in the short term was Nur ad-Din, for Shirkuh died almost at the moment of his triumph, and Nur was able to control Egypt through his representative Saladin. In 1171, on Nur's orders and after the death of the unfortunate al-'Adid, the Fatimid caliphate was suppressed. Shi'ite rule in Egypt, after two hundred years, was over and one of the aims of Nur's jihad – the extension of Sunni orthodoxy – had been furthered significantly. But Nur proved unable to control his protégé, who had adopted the Seljuq title of sultan in Egypt. By 1174, Nur was ready to call Saladin to account for his governance in Egypt when he died following a short illness after a game of polo.

The way was clear for Saladin to assume full control in Egypt, but the Kurd was not content with that. He realized that despite the widespread authority Nur had commanded throughout Syria, his dynastic hold was precarious. His heir, as-Salih, was only eleven years old; one nephew, Saif ad-Din, who controlled Mosul, began openly to flout Nur's example of pious rulership by riotous living; his other nephew, 'Imad ad-Din Zengi, barely clung to power in Sinjar. Saladin used the pretext of an anticipated Frankish invasion of Damascus to march a small army to Syria himself. He was doubly fortunate: the Syrian emirs who wanted to control as-Salih were divided among themselves, and in July 1174 King Amalric died, leaving an uncertain succession in Jerusalem. Saladin's prompt action caught prospective opponents in Damascus on the back foot, and he was invited to take control of the city on behalf of as-Salih. At least one Arab chronicler later wrote that he had bought off opposition with handsome payments, and William of Tyre, a canny observer from Jerusalem, remarked that one of the things that made Saladin so dangerous was his generosity. As-Salih was whisked off to Aleppo by emirs loyal to the Zengid dynasty, and it was from Aleppo that the only challenge to what was obviously a *coup d'état* came. Qutb ad-Din, one of Nur's emirs, sent the message that the swords that had given Saladin Egypt would drive him back there. Although Saladin took an army into north Syria and secured the surrender of Homs, he could not make any impression on Aleppo's strong defences and withdrew. It would not be until 1183 that he would be able to conquer the city.

Saladin was the first Muslim leader to control Damascus and Egypt at the same time. This gave him strategic advantages that previous Seljuq rulers had not enjoyed. The kingdom of Jerusalem, for the first time since its foundation, was confronted by an enemy who could surround it. During the course of the next twenty years or so, Saladin would demonstrate more than once how his command of the routes to the east of the Jordan enabled him to bypass the kingdom, moving armies quickly from one power base to another. He presented the most serious threat the Frankish settlers had yet faced. But his control of Syria, and his standing in the Muslim world as a whole, was far from assured. The fact that he was a Kurd, rather than a member of the Seljuq aristocracy, counted against him. He was relatively unknown outside Egypt, and his takeover in Damascus was a clear breach of the dynastic succession of the powerful Zengid clan. Although the Abbasid caliphate wielded no effective power, caliphs were still important figureheads in Sunni Islam, especially when it came to questions of legitimacy to rule. Nur's legitimacy was accepted partly because he was the son of Zengi, but also because of his personal qualifications as a pious Muslim. In this respect, Saladin was still an unknown quantity.

He would remain so until he could demonstrate that he shared Nur's jihad ideals, and this meant taking on the Franks. In his first three years in power in Syria, however, the holy war had no place at all. By 1177, things had changed, and he was spurred into action by the arrival in the kingdom of Jerusalem of Philip, count of Flanders, with a large army. At first it looked as though it would be a defensive war, for the Byzantine emperor Manuel Komnenos had proposed a joint invasion of Egypt with a Byzantine fleet to support a Frankish land army, but Philip balked at taking on the same problems that had proved too difficult for Amalric to overcome ten years earlier. Instead, with support from the anti-Byzantine regent of Jerusalem, Raymond of Tripoli, Philip took his army into north Syria, leaving the kingdom defended only by the sixteen-year-old leper king, Baldwin IV, and a few barons under Reynald of Châtillon. It looked like a perfect opportunity to carry the holy war to the Franks, and Saladin ought to have won a decisive victory. But at the Battle of Montgisard near Gaza, Saladin was outmanoeuvred by Reynald and forced off the field. The Franks were not numerous enough to press the advantage; had they had a stronger force, it could have spelled an end to Saladin's ambitions. As it was, a year later Saladin appeared with an army in the north of the kingdom, having circled it from the south and east, and attacked the newly built Templar castle of Jacob's Ford.

Saladin had still not made much of an impression on contemporaries as a jihad leader. Opinion was divided on his rule in Egypt. His secretary, 'Imad ad-Din, later painted a portrait of Saladin as conscientious, pious and sober, and this was amplified by his biographer, Ibn Shaddad, but in Egypt he had his critics. One of them, Al-Wahrani, accused Saladin of not being a real Muslim at all, and bitterly criticized his appointment of Kurds to positions of authority. It was not until after 1183 that Saladin began to claim the moral high ground with any conviction. This year marked a new stage in his career. He finally captured Aleppo, assuring his control over two of the three main centres of power in Syria. Later in the year, he invaded the kingdom of Jerusalem again, this time with serious intent. It was an opportunity handed to him by the actions of Reynald of Châtillon. In the previous year, Reynald, whose fief lay across the Jordan in the desert to the east of the Dead Sea, had taken a small force carrying collapsible boats on camels south to the Gulf of Aqaba, where they launched a series of raids on the Red Sea coastal towns. Saladin was able to counter the raid swiftly, and Frankish captives were paraded in Cairo before being executed, but the real value for him lay in the propaganda he could generate from it. Reynald may not seriously have been attempting to threaten the holy cities of Mecca and Medina, but his raid demonstrated their vulnerability, and Saladin's robust defence enabled him to present himself as the protector of Islam. When he invaded the Galilee in 1183, it was as an act of revenge for this insult. Although this invasion came to nothing, he employed the same tactic three years later when Reynald raided a caravan conveying pilgrims to Mecca; according to some later writers, among the pilgrims was Saladin's own sister, whom Reynald took prisoner. This time it was not only an insult to Islamic pilgrimage, but to Saladin's own family. As in 1183, Saladin's invasion of 1187 followed a major success over a Muslim opponent: in 1183, over Aleppo; in 1186, over Mosul. During the intervening years Saladin's secretariat had worked hard to reconstruct Saladin's image. The 'jihad of the tongue' continued to pour out of his offices as it had from Nur ad-Din's, and Saladin kept the caliph constantly informed of his actions and the intentions behind them. That it worked is made clear from reading the pilgrimage account of 1184, written by the Spanish Muslim Ibn Jubayr. Brought up in the Almohad regime in Andalusia, Ibn Jubayr was well used to jihad ideals. To him, Saladin was an authentic hero of the jihad, who deserved the support of the whole Islamic world.

It was this kind of support that enabled Saladin to assemble the coalition of forces with which he invaded the kingdom again in the spring of 1187. Emirs with their followers and paid troops not only from Egypt and Mesopotamia but as far afield as Yemen joined him. The victory at Hattin made possible the annexation of most of the kingdom, but it was the recapture of Jerusalem in October 1187 that marked the real purpose of the campaign and gave meaning to Saladin's career to that point. As one contemporary writer put it, the holy city had been cleansed by the blood of the infidels. Jerusalem was transformed almost overnight into an Islamic city: most of the churches, with the exception of the Holy Sepulchre, were converted into mosques, and the Dome of the Rock, which had become an Augustinian monastery, and al-Aqsa mosque, which had been given to the Knights Templar in 1119, were reclaimed for Islam.

In his triumphant campaign of 1187–8, Saladin might have been excused for the single military failure represented by his inability to capture the city of Tyre. But it was from this failure that the Third Crusade was given a foothold. Many of the surviving Franks crowded into the city, whose defences were organized by Conrad of Montferrat, a north Italian baron who had sailed to the Holy Land, hoping to help the Christian cause, just as Acre had fallen to Saladin. Guy of Lusignan, who had been captured at Hattin, was released in 1188 through Saladin's extraordinary clemency. Two years after Hattin, he tried to resume command of the Franks, but was rebuffed by Conrad at Tyre. In a move that smacks of desperation, he took a small following of knights and foot soldiers to begin what looked like a hopeless siege of Acre. Perhaps because Saladin did not take it seriously at first, the siege grew as more of the Franks joined it, and it provided a focal point for the gathering of crusaders from the West enthused by the preaching of a new expedition by Pope Gregory VIII in 1188. Although this crusade was to be led by three kings – the German emperor Frederick Barbarossa, Philip II of France and Richard I of England – sizeable groups of crusaders from all over Europe began to assemble at Acre before the royal armies finally arrived in 1191. The kings had been delayed. Richard could only leave once his father Henry II's death had brought an end to hostilities with Philip of France, but even after they had both set out together there were further delays en route. The first of these occurred in Sicily, where Richard had dynastic business relating to his sister Joanna's marriage into the royal house. After the death of her husband, William II, Joanna's dowry was retained illegally by the new king, William's cousin Tancred. Richard allowed his troops to riot in Messina until a proper financial settlement had been reached. A further delay occurred in Cyprus after the army had set out again. The ship carrying Richard's fiancée, who was travelling with the crusade, was blown into port at Cyprus during a storm, and the Byzantine ruler of the island, Isaac Komnenos, thought he could improve his position by holding her for ransom. Instead he found his island being taken from him in a whirlwind campaign by Richard. Consequently it was not until the summer of 1191 that Richard finally reached Acre, by which time the siege had been going on for two years. The German contingent proved much smaller in the end than had been anticipated, because disaster had struck in Asia Minor. Marching overland, Frederick Barbarossa drowned trying to cross a river in Cilicia in June 1190. Much of his army disintegrated once it reached Antioch, and his son Frederick of Swabia died during the siege of Acre. The *coup de grâce* to the siege was supplied by Richard and Philip, but much of the preliminary work of undermining and weakening the city's defences, while fending off Saladin's forays against them, had already been done by the besiegers, led initially by Guy.

The fall of Acre to Richard and Philip was another turning point in Saladin's career. Even though the crusade turned out to be smaller in size than he had feared – and diminished still further when Philip II left the Holy Land after Acre – Saladin was too wary of Richard to tackle him in open battle. His only attempt to do so, an ambush on the coastal plain at Arsuf, between Caesarea and Jaffa, in September 1191, ended in a decisive defeat. The loss of morale at this defeat was clear to Muslim observers. 'We were wounded in heart and in body', mourned Ibn Shaddad. Even earlier, many of the emirs who had joined Saladin from far-flung regions of the *umma* began to leave his service during the siege of Acre. The spell he had seemed to cast over Muslims was losing its force. He was unable to prevent Richard's recapture of Jaffa and Ascalon, and a year of see-saw fighting between Arsuf and Richard's final departure in October 1192 resulted in the restoration of enough of the kingdom of Jerusalem to the Franks to make it once again a viable political unit, based on Acre and Tyre and hugging the coastline. Of course, the ultimate goal of the crusade was the recovery of Jerusalem, but a combination of canny strategy and luck kept Saladin in control of the holy city. Richard was twice within reach of Jerusalem, in the winter of 1191–2 and again in June 1192, but on neither occasion did he consider that he had the necessary combination of favourable

Figure 5   The capture of Acre on the Third Crusade, 1191. The leading knight in the picture is the king of France, Philip Augustus. (Source: From a fourteenth-century manuscript of the *Chroniques de France*, British Library Royal MS 16 G.VI, f. 352v.)

weather conditions and sufficient troops to embark on a siege. The crusade was also hampered by political infighting. Conrad of Montferrat's intriguing for the throne, which achieved shortlived success in 1192, deprived the crusade of the unity between crusaders and native Franks that was needed. But in military terms, the crusade showed that a defender who was prepared to ride the storm, delay crusaders as long as possible and withdraw in the face of superior force, would always have the advantage. By the time he had been in the East for eighteen months, Richard could no longer afford the time or energy to pursue the crusade. He had realized that if crusades did not make an immediate military impact, they were unlikely wholly to succeed.

Saladin's reputation fell temporarily as a result of the Third Crusade. Although he had clung on to Jerusalem, he had been outfought more than once by Richard. He continued to press his fellow Muslims to greater efforts for the jihad, but there were already signs that these ideals were dwindling. His brother Al-'Adil, who succeeded him, would show little of Saladin's fervour for holy war. Yet Saladin had achieved what no previous Muslim ruler had done since the seventh century, and he impressed contemporaries among both Muslims and Christians by the force of his personality. He had critics among Muslims, as he has among modern historians, but he was also loved and respected. Whatever the route by which he came to power, from 1183 onwards, he appeared to embody the ideals of the good Muslim ruler. As his contemporary biographer Ibn Shaddad listed them, his virtues as a ruler and a man conformed to the essentials of Islam: he was regular in his observance of both prayer and fasts; he gave alms generously and instituted an alms tax in Egypt; and he was unyielding in his pursuit of holy war. What impressed Christians as well as Muslims was his quality of mercy. At Acre, when a group of newly arrived pilgrims from the West fell into his hands as prisoners, he freed them and let them go on their way to Jerusalem out of respect for the piety that had brought them so far. When the mother of a Christian child who had been captured by his soldiers came to him in tears, he ordered the release of the child and paid the ransom out of his own pocket. Incidents such as these made him an authentically heroic figure, much lauded as a 'chivalrous' character in his own day. His reputation was fully revived by nineteenth-century romantics in the West and by Arab nationalists in the Middle East, and in the twenty-first century he far outstrips his mentor, Nur ad-Din, in fame.

6

Pope Innocent III: the crusading pope

The Third Crusade had left the job, begun in 1187, less than half done. Although the city of Jerusalem was still in Turkish hands, some of the rest of the kingdom's territory, notably the city of Acre, had been reconquered. A large number of fiefs, however, were still in enemy hands. To some extent these losses were offset by the acquisition of Cyprus by Richard I, which gave knightly families who had lost their lands in 1187 the opportunity to recover their fortunes at the expense of the Greek natives of the island. The vigorous if brief rule over the kingdom of Jerusalem by Henry of Champagne (1192–7) did much to restore royal authority, helped by a succession crisis among the Ayyubids after Saladin's death. Moreover, the coastal strip that had been reconquered, comprising the fertile plains of Acre and Tyre, represented the most agriculturally productive parts of the old kingdom, while the loss of territory also had the consequence that towns such as Acre and Tyre grew from the influx of displaced landowners. The crown seems to have granted fresh urban fiefs – based on grants of money rather than land – after 1192, which indicates that its resources were recovering from the disaster of 1187.

Although the fond hope of Pope Celestine III, expressed in a bull of January 1193, was that another expedition would be launched to complete the task by recovering Jerusalem itself, few practical steps were taken. It fell instead to the son of Frederick Barbarossa, Henry VI, to reinvigorate crusading. As emperor and master of the kingdom of Sicily, which his wife Constance had inherited in 1189, Henry was a formidable figure. Moreover, he had also acquired an interest in Cyprus. Richard I had given his conquest to Guy of Lusignan, but retained nominal overlordship of the island. During his return to the West via the land route, Richard was captured by Leopold, duke of Austria. Leopold, related by marriage to the dispossessed Isaac Komnenos, saw a chance for revenge, but his own lord, Henry VI, took over his royal prisoner, to be released only in 1194 on payment of a huge ransom and transfer of his overlordship of Cyprus. Henry's crusade was to have been entirely his own. Though endorsed by the papacy, it owed nothing to specific papal preaching or encouragement, and Henry seems to have seen the expedition as a way of cementing his own authority on an international stage – demanding, for instance, provisions and armed support from the Byzantines. In the event, Henry never made it to the Holy Land, dying in September 1197. His crusade is worthy of mention, however, for three reasons. First, because the advance forces that arrived in spring 1197 managed, in concert with the Franks of the East, to retake Beirut and thus to continue the reconsolidation of the kingdom's territory. More significant is the fact that Henry's expedition represents the first autonomous crusade undertaken by a lay ruler without reference to the papacy. Previous kings, such as Sigurd of Norway, and plenty of high-ranking nobles had led their own private armed expeditions to the East, but Henry not only organized such an expedition: he expected, as emperor, that it would be endorsed and preached by the pope, and that the customary spiritual privileges would be offered to his followers. It was an important precedent. A third feature of the crusade is the light it sheds on the changed relationship between the kingdom of Jerusalem and the Western powers. The treaty made in 1197 between the new king of Jerusalem, Aimery of Lusignan, and Saladin's successor, al-Adil, allowed for the five-year truce to be broken by the Muslims if a powerful Christian king arrived in the East. This, effectively, demonstrated how weak the kingdom of Jerusalem was in the 1190s. Whatever policy it adopted towards the Ayyubids could be automatically overturned by the arrival of a new crusade.

The assumption by Henry VI that the pope would endorse his crusading plans, and thus that crusading depended on his initiative rather than the papacy's, may have persuaded Celestine III's successor to change crusading policy profoundly. Innocent III came to the papal throne in 1198 at the age of only thirty-seven. He was already an experienced manager with expertise both in canon law and the regulation of religious communities, but his spirituality and personal piety were also recognized by contemporaries. He made the crusade the keynote of his eighteen-year pontificate, but although he preached and authorized more crusading activity than any of his predecessors, and changed the way in which crusades were planned and organized, his legacy was mixed.

Innocent began by trying to continue the German crusade, and preachers were commissioned to recruit in France and England. Some success was achieved in the Loire and Saône regions of France, in Flanders and Champagne, where the counts took the cross, and in Germany. But no kings were recruited. Was this because Innocent thought that the business of the crusade was for popes rather than kings to manage and feared that a powerful king would undermine his authority? This is plausible, given Innocent's very high conception of the dignity of the papal office. But it is also the case that no kings were available in 1098. Henry VI's death left the Empire at the mercy of three claimants, including his three-year-old son, Frederick, who was also the heir to Sicily. Richard died in the midst of war against Capetian France in 1199, leaving the Angevin dominions to be disputed between his brother John and his nephew. In these circumstances, Philip II himself was clearly also unavailable, since as king of France he had a keen interest in the Angevin succession crisis.

The practical management of the crusade was left to the major barons who had taken the cross. They appointed a committee of six to negotiate with the republic of Venice the transport of the crusaders to the East. The agreement made early in 1201 was that the Venetians would spend a year building a fleet sufficient to transport 4,500 knights and their horses, 9,000 squires and 20,000 foot soldiers. Venice was a major maritime commercial power, but its ships were designed to carry freight, not horses and armed men, so a huge construction programme had to be set in train. In addition, the Venetians agreed to contribute fifty war galleys with armed men, the whole to cost the crusaders 85,000 marks – a huge sum that corresponds to about £30 million sterling today. As far as we can tell, this was a competitive price, for example when compared with what Richard I had paid the Genoese to charter ships for his expedition in 1191. Things began to go awry when the count of Champagne, who was to have led the crusade, died in spring 1201. This may also have meant the loss of substantial forces. His replacement was Boniface, marquis of Montferrat. This choice was to remove the strategic organization of the crusade from the hands of the baronial committee to the sphere of international politics. Boniface was from a family with an incomparable crusading pedigree. Two older brothers, William Longsword and Conrad, had been married to heiresses to the throne of Jerusalem; Boniface's nephew Baldwin V had even sat on the throne in 1186. A third, Renier, had married a Komnena princess in Constantinople. But Boniface's involvement also pulled in his lord, Philip, duke of Swabia, one of the rival claimants to the imperial throne. This was because in 1201–2 Philip was hosting his brother-in-law, the Byzantine prince Alexios IV. Alexios was the son of the former emperor Isaac II Angelos, who had been deposed and blinded by his brother Alexios III in 1195. Father and son were placed under house arrest, but Alexios escaped and went to the West to seek help in putting his father back on the throne. Boniface appears to have met Alexios at Philip's court and to have agreed to the justice of his cause, though probably without at this stage committing himself to anything further. Alexios lobbied the other prominent crusading nobles as they were travelling to Venice, but he seems to have been ignored.

By June 1202, however, the crusade was in trouble. The date set for meeting the terms of the agreement with Venice passed with less than half of the crusaders present, and this of course meant that the money owed could not be paid. The money collected by papal preachers had been sent directly to the Holy Land to pay for the repair of fortifications, and only 51,000 marks could be raised from the crusaders at Venice. The Venetians and crusaders were at an impasse. The crusaders could not return home without being released from their vows, while the Venetians could not afford to write off the loss of a year's shipbuilding for less than the sum agreed. Time was pressing, for while the Venetians did not want a poorly supplied army sitting idle in the city, nor could they afford to provide food and fodder for nothing. The solution proposed by the Doge of Venice, Enrico Dandolo, was radical and far-reaching. He himself took the cross and encouraged other Venetians to do the same. The combined crusading army would go to war, but instead of sailing as planned straight to Egypt, it would first seize back the Venetian trading post of Zara (now Zadar) on the Adriatic coast of Croatia, which had been taken by the king of Hungary. The inconvenient fact that Zara was now in the hands of a Christian king who had himself taken the cross, and that the crusaders would thus be fulfilling their vows in war against a fellow crusader, was overridden by the extreme need of the situation. The papal legate was caught in a dilemma: the action proposed, though illegal, was the only way to keep the crusade going.

In the event, Zara was duly taken, but only at the expense of some of the crusaders, who refused to join the siege. Moreover, Innocent's response to the assault on a crusader's possession was to excommunicate the Venetians. This meant that by winter 1202 the crusade was becalmed. It could go no further without ships, but the Venetians had been excommunicated and could therefore no longer participate in the crusade. It was at this point that Alexios IV intervened by offering to underwrite the crusade to the tune of 200,000 marks, supplies and a ten-thousand-strong army – unimaginable riches – but only on condition that the crusaders first divert from their original destination of Egypt and restore his father Isaac II and himself jointly to the Byzantine throne. They might then use his wealth to go on to the Holy Land or Egypt. Some crusaders refused outright and left Zara at this point, but the majority accepted that they had no choice if the crusade were not to collapse. In April 1203, therefore, the expedition set sail on a new course: Constantinople.

Presumably Alexios either knew that the Byzantine defences were weaker than they appeared or counted on popular support from his people for the restoration of the rightful emperor. At first it looked as though his calculations were correct. The crusaders occupied Galata, on the northern side of the Golden Horn, without real opposition, and their first assault on the city by land and sea on 17 July scared Alexios III into abandoning it. Although Byzantine military strength was not what it had been even a generation earlier, the defence of the city could have been more tenacious. The crusaders had to divide their forces into a seaborne assault led by Venetian ships against the city walls in the south-west of the Golden Horn and an attack on the fifth-century land walls that guarded the west of the city. In both actions the outcome was in the balance, and better leadership might have swung the battle in the Byzantines' favour. Alexios III led a force far superior to the crusaders' outside the walls to meet their assault. According to Robert of Clari, an eyewitness, the emperor had seventeen divisions to the crusaders' seven, but he inexplicably withdrew his forces from resisting the land-based attack just when it looked as though the crusaders would be driven off. Probably he had simply not believed that the Venetian assault from the sea could work and panicked when he realized he was under attack on two fronts.

Isaac was restored to the throne, to rule alongside his son. This should have been the cue for the crusaders to be paid off and depart to fulfil their crusade vows. In the event, he was unable to find the money he had promised in the imperial treasury, and the Byzantines themselves became increasingly disillusioned with his attempts to acquire more by looting church treasures and raising taxes. In February 1204, Alexios IV was killed in a riot and replaced by a Byzantine noble, Alexios Mourtzouphlos, who proved to be fiercely opposed to the crusaders and indeed all Westerners. The crusaders decided to take matters into their own hands – by attacking the city again and taking for themselves what they were owed. In April 1204 they broke through the defences; Constantinople was theirs. One reason why the Fourth Crusade has a bad name is what then ensued. Churches, palaces and houses were looted of relics, treasures and works of art systematically and apparently without regard for either piety or aesthetic sensibilities. Both Western and Byzantine eyewitnesses were awestruck at the scale of the pillaging, though in the case of the former, part of the awe was doubtless that so much could be contained in one city.

One of the crusade leaders, Geoffrey of Villehardouin, a knight from Champagne, wrote an account of the expedition. He explained why he thought the crusade had taken the course that it had. The reason for the lack of sufficient funds to pay the Venetians in 1202 was that some crusaders, ignoring or ignorant of the agreement made by the crusade's leaders with Venice, had made their own transport arrangements and left from ports other than Venice. Villehardouin blamed these crusaders for the events of 1202–4, and defended the decisions of the leaders at every stage on the grounds that the only other option would have been to abandon the crusade. The intended end – the recovery of Jerusalem – justified any means used to achieve it. Moreover, he insisted, right up to the final assault on Constantinople the intention was still simply to collect the resources needed to get the crusaders to Egypt. This protestation is somewhat undermined by the fact that the leaders had agreed on a division of the Empire with the Venetians before the assault took place. In any event, once Constantinople had fallen and the regime of Mourtzouphlos had been disbanded, the business of filling the power vacuum put paid to any completion of the crusade. Baldwin, count of Flanders, was elected emperor; Boniface received the fief once owned by his brother Renier, Thessaloniki; and the Venetians took control of the Aegean islands and Crete.

The Fourth Crusade gives out mixed signals to those looking for lessons from its result. Poor communications and logistical organization, and possibly also weak leadership, resulted, as Villehardouin realized, in the initial problem of the crusaders failing to co-ordinate their journeys. This, rather than the terms of the agreement with Venice, scuppered the crusade. Furthermore, papal leadership was exposed as a chimera once Innocent was faced with the dilemma at Zara. The standard spiritual weapon of excommunication proved inadequate as a threat and as a punishment. On the other hand, in purely military terms, the crusade was astonishingly successful: to take a city of the size of Constantinople, even one relatively poorly led, was a considerable achievement. To have achieved it with a quite small army, with pre-carious supplies and without the machinery of royal government is testament to the potency of the western European baronage as a military force. Success could also be claimed in another way. Innocent III had, like previous popes, tried diplomacy to bring the Orthodox Church of Byzantium to accept papal primacy. As with efforts made by previous popes, his arguments had no effect. Yet the crusade, though pursued to a military conclusion against his will, had brought about exactly the result that he and previous popes had wanted. In the aftermath of conquest, a Venetian cleric, Thomas of Lentini, was appointed patriarch of Constantinople, and the Latin liturgy was sung in St Sophia and other churches throughout the city and Empire.

Even so, for Innocent III, the result of the crusade was embarrassing. He had lost control of events and been unable to act effectively through his legate, Peter Capuano, to stop an assault on a crusader by crusaders. The crusade's freedom of action had been constrained by a financial mechanism that had remained basically unchanged since 1095. The dependence of the crusade on individual crusaders paying their own head-money exposed the flaws of a system in which individuals or groups were not bound to an overall strategy. Innocent decided that two remedies were needed: the centralization of financing and tighter control of crusading vows. Over the course of the next decade, both of these reforms were set in place, with effects that would prove lasting throughout the Middle Ages.

The idea of a special tax to finance a crusade was not new, and the participation of Richard I and Philip II in the Third Crusade had been financed through a tax known as the 'Saladin tithe'. In the Middle Ages, taxes were imposed irregularly and only in certain circumstances, because even the wealthy did not necessarily have the liquid capital needed to pay out large sums of money annually. In a predominantly agricultural economy, wealth was tied up in land, and the only class of people who had what might be seen as a regular salaried income were the clergy, who were paid a tithe (literally, a tenth) of the income of their parishioners. Tithes, like rent, might be in coin or in kind. Priests kept back part of the tithe for their upkeep and that of the parish church; the rest was collected for the running of the diocese. Innocent authorized the use of tithes to fund crusading operations: effectively, the diversion of Church funds for a particular operation of the Church. In principle, a crusading tithe could be announced at any time, to be collected for a given period – say, three years – from the incomes of all clergy in Christendom. Each bishop was responsible for collection in his diocese, and the sums were to be forwarded to Rome, there to be assigned for use by the pope. Of course, the crusading tithe was a highly political tool. In authorizing

the collection and use of clerical incomes in this way, the pope
was asserting his authority to control all income accruing to the
Church, and thus overriding the local authority of bishops. He
was also claiming the authority to determine the direction and
policy of a crusade. Innocent III was to show that he was fully
alive to the implications of both these points.

We have already seen that around the year 1200, the status of
those who took the cross was changing. More fixed privileges
and conditions meant that to be a crusader was to occupy a legal
category within canon law. It was especially important in these
circumstances that those who took the cross should be seen to
have fulfilled their vows by actually going on crusade. Early-
thirteenth-century records show localized attempts to audit participation by recording the vows of those who took the cross and
then checking that they had joined a crusade. Part of the problem
was that anyone could take the cross at any time, regardless of
whether a crusade had been preached for a particular purpose or
at a particular time. This meant that there were people with the
status of crusader – like King Emico of Hungary in 1203 – who
had not yet done anything to merit it. A king, like Henry II of
England in 1171, might take the cross as an act of penance and
find himself unable for reasons of state to undertake an expedition, yet try to fulfil his vows by sending money or troops to the
kingdom of Jerusalem. Innocent III took this kind of precedent
as the basis for a new system of vow-redemption. The idea was
that everyone was encouraged to take the cross, regardless of
social status or fitness for military action. Those who could not
fulfil their vows because of poverty, illness, family commitments
or the like could then redeem them by the payment of a sum of
money. Vow-redemption money was then collected centrally in
each diocese, to be sent on to Rome or wherever directed by the
pope. As with the crusading tax, it was a means of centralizing
papal authority while at the same time achieving two practical outcomes: raising more money for crusading, obviously, but

also involving the wider Christian community in the project of the crusade. In this way crusading was, in principle at least, not only the business of kings and nobles, or even of knights and foot soldiers, but also of pious townspeople, well-to-do peasants, clergy and women. It meant a re-focusing of the meaning of the crusade to the centre of Christian life, reinforced by Innocent's encouragement of regular crusade preaching in all dioceses and public processions at which the cross was carried as a reminder of the fate of Jerusalem.

The growing institutionalization of crusading made possible an increase in crusading activity. In particular it meant that when religious problems arose in the West that required a political as well as a spiritual solution, the crusade filled the need. Such an

Figure 6   Saladin's soldiers lead Christians into captivity as the city of Jerusalem burns. (Source: From a thirteenth-century French manuscript of the *Histoire d'Outremer*, comprising William of Tyre's *Chronicle* with continuations up to 1332, British Library Yates Thompson MS 12, f.161.)

occasion occurred in 1209 in south-western France. For about half a century, unorthodox beliefs had been spreading throughout this region and in the towns of northern Italy. The most important of these beliefs was Catharism. Originally from the Balkans, Catharism was a dualist faith that claimed to be the truest form of Christianity. Cathars believed that the universe was split into two spheres: the spiritual, governed by God, and the material, governed by the Devil. Cathars believed that created matter was essentially the province of the Devil, but that humans, having souls, were spiritual beings trapped in created matter. The purpose of religion was to free the soul to its proper home, the spiritual sphere. Cathars rejected the main teachings of the Church, and especially the sacraments. Since they held that Jesus could not have been divine, they did not believe in the Resurrection, and without this central tenet of Christian belief, there was no need for the edifice of the Church at all.

Historians today are in disagreement over the degree to which all Cathars held these extreme views. Part of the problem is that very little written evidence of Cathar beliefs survives except in sources compiled by clergy acting against Cathars. Many laypeople in southern France – a region with its own language and distinctive cultural traditions – were probably attracted to Catharism to a greater or lesser degree because of dissatisfaction with the levels of education and performance of their own clergy. Moreover, support for Catharism became a strategy of opposition. Once the papacy had identified Catharism as an enemy of Christianity, Cathars and those suspected of harbouring or supporting them were targeted by both organized preaching and spiritual deterrents such as excommunication. In 1182, Pope Lucius III and Emperor Frederick I issued a joint bull authorizing the use of force to compel Cathars and other heretics to accept punishment for the good of the whole Christian community. The intent behind this was probably to take action against individuals or small groups of heretics to compel them to abjure their beliefs. Until 1209, however, there had been no systematic use of force on a large scale. The strategy employed by the Church was twofold. First, preaching campaigns were undertaken throughout areas where Catharism was prevalent. In addition, the most prominent noble in the region, Raymond VI, count of Toulouse, was required by the papacy to suppress Catharism in lands under his control. That neither worked shows how little the papacy understood on the one hand the deficiencies of those appointed to preach for the task at hand, and on the other the social structures of power in the region. Raymond, though not himself a Cathar, did not have either the authority or the mechanisms of government to hand to root out Catharism. In 1209, after Peter of Castelnau, one of the papal legates sent to bolster papal authority, had been murdered by one of Raymond's knights, Innocent preached a crusade against Raymond.

Innocent's use of the crusade as a tool to counter heresy may appear revolutionary. Warfare was being sanctioned by the papacy against an enemy within rather than against an external threat. In fact, this was a logical step from Innocent's point of view. Just as Islamic possession of Jerusalem could be seen as a threat to the territorial integrity of Christendom (or what was thought by Christians *should* be Christendom), so heresy presented a threat to the integrity of Christian society. The language that was typically used by popes and preachers to describe heresy – it was a disease, a cancer, a wound – indicates the mindset of the Church. Heresy could not be allowed to continue, because just as an untreated wound in the leg of an otherwise healthy man would fester and infect the rest of the body, so Christian society, which represented the body of Christ in the world, would become infected if heresy were left untreated. And if heretics could not be persuaded to abjure wrong beliefs, then there was no option but to compel them by force or to get rid of them.

The problem of heresy thus took on a military dimension, but it became no easier to resolve. For one thing, whereas in taking on the Turks who held Jerusalem or the Arabs in Spain, a crusade army had an easily identifiable target, this was not the case in southern France. Citizens of towns like Albi or Narbonne, where Catharism was known to be strong, were just as likely to find themselves victims of military assault as were known Cathar landowners. The Albigensian Crusade, as it is known, came to be a war of the largely northern French nobility who took the cross against Occitan speakers of the region south of the Gironde and the Garonne. It was a war of shifting fortunes, as local lords and key strategic targets were identified and attacked one after another. The initial phase of the war (1209–11) saw the annexation of the lands of the supposed Cathar sympathizer Raymond Trenceval, followed by the dismantling of the county of Toulouse. Count Raymond VI, who had acquiesced in the attack on his vassal Trenceval in order to evade the crusade, now found himself its target, but between 1216 and 1225 the southern French barons mounted an effective resistance, taking back several strongholds and bringing the crusade to a halt. By 1229, more or less the whole region had come under the control of the French crown, because of the participation of Philip II's heir, Louis VIII. Although he had participated in the campaigning in 1215 and 1219, once he was king he pursued the war with vigour, and his invasion of the Languedoc in 1226 eventually proved decisive.

How revolutionary was the Albigensian Crusade? Force had been encouraged against those who resisted or opposed papal authority since the mid–eleventh century. Pope Gregory VII had tried to deploy force both to defend Rome against the armies of Emperor Henry IV and against 'enemies of reform' in Italian towns such as Milan. In one sense, Urban II was building on this when he preached the crusade in 1095, so one might see his expedition as a particular application of the more general principle of the just war. But there was a difference between declaring that a particular struggle, which might involve force, was justifiable or even righteous, and actively recruiting soldiers on the basis that it was a penance for sins they had committed. The first guaranteed that the justification would be taken into consideration; the second substituted killing for temporal acts of penance. The Albigensian Crusade encouraged the killing of those identified as heretics or supporters of heresy as a penance for the sins of the knighthood.

The Albigensian Crusade had yet to achieve anything when Innocent died in 1216. Another ongoing project was the crusade for the recovery of Jerusalem, which Innocent first announced in 1213. The Fifth Crusade was intended to bear the fruit of the reforms implemented since 1204. In contrast to the delegation of authority in the planning of the Fourth Crusade, Innocent retained full control of the organization for the Fifth. In 1215, during a papal council designed to implement a host of reforms in the Church, he announced the proposed date of departure for crusaders travelling by land and sea; the destination, Egypt; financial measures to be taken to ensure the crusade was properly funded; and other details of planning, including a ban on trade with Muslim-held ports. The years after 1204 had been largely peaceful in the Crusader States, since the Seljuk ruler al-Adil was content to renew the truce. From 1211, however, a more febrile atmosphere seems to have arisen, perhaps as a result of apocalyptic expectations throughout Christendom and among Jewish communities in Europe.

The degree to which this climate of expectation, coupled with Innocent's promotion of crusading, succeeded in infusing the European imagination can be seen from the curious phenomenon of 1212, known as the Children's Crusade. In late spring, groups of young people in northern France and western Germany began to follow the Rhine south towards Italy. Most of the French groups probably dispersed before reaching the south, but many of the Germans, led by a youth named Nicholas, were found wandering in the Italian ports from which pilgrims and crusaders typically embarked for the Holy Land. Local chronicles report that when asked what they were doing, the young men and women replied that they were going to retake Jerusalem. What battle-hardened knights had been unable to do would be accomplished by the innocent and defenceless. Most of the youths were probably unemployed day labourers in their teens, used to migrating around the countryside to find work in season. Whether they really believed in their charismatic leader or were simply looking for adventure, the groups broke up when they realized the impossibility of getting across the Mediterranean, let alone achieving their aim. Some, like Nicholas himself, appear to have been genuinely motivated by a spirit of popular piety.

The Fifth Crusade did not finally get under way until June 1217, some months after Innocent's death. Innocent had wanted the crusade to be an enterprise of the whole of Christendom, and crusade armies from Holland, various regions of Germany, Hungary, northern Italy, France and England joined the Franks of Cyprus and the kingdom of Jerusalem over the course of four years in a series of staggered departures. The first campaign was the demolition of a Muslim fortress on Mount Tabor, in Galilee, but the main thrust of the crusade was to be the invasion of Egypt. The calculation that Egypt, the powerhouse of the Ayyubid regime, was the real gateway to Jerusalem, had been made as early as 1192. Al-Adil could not ignore an attack on the heartland of his rule and might have been prepared to sacrifice Jerusalem if it meant saving Cairo and Alexandria. Moreover, Egypt was thought to be a relatively easy target, since it was flat, had few fortified towns or castles and offered an easy passage across the Sinai Peninsula to the Holy Land. One of those fortified towns, however, was the crusaders' first target, Damietta. Guarding the mouth of the Nile, Damietta was defended by a triple rampart and a tower from which a chain stretched across the river. Once past this obstacle, however, the crusaders would, in theory, find the path to Cairo via the Nile open to them.

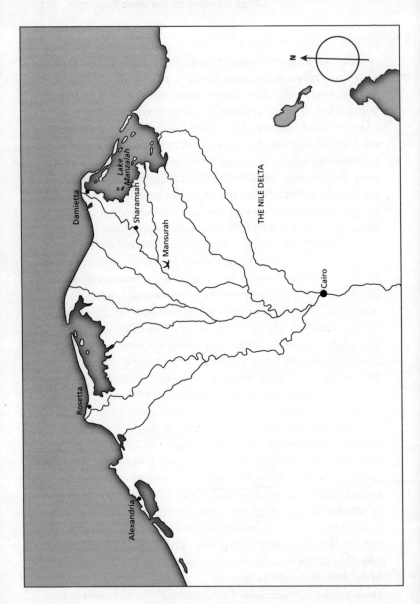

Map 3: The Nile Delta

It took fourteen months to take Damietta: an arduous and expensive campaign by land and sea. It was during the siege that St Francis of Assisi, still relatively unknown at that time outside Italy, made a dramatic appearance in Egypt with the intention of converting the sultan to Christianity and thereby obviating the need for violence. Although the sultan allowed him to preach before him, he gave no sign of being swayed by Francis' obvious piety and sincerity. Even before the city fell in November 1219, the Ayyubids had offered the crusaders exactly the terms that they had apparently wanted. Al-Kamil, who had succeeded his father al-Adil as sultan in Egypt, undertook to return not only Jerusalem itself, but the full territorial extent of the kingdom as it had been in 1187, except for the two Transjordan fortresses of Kerak and Montreal, on condition that they abandon Egypt. Why did the crusaders not accept the deal that offered everything for which they had fought so hard? The divisions among the ranks of the crusaders revealed by this moment of crisis go a long way to explaining the ultimate failure of the crusade as a whole. Leadership had been an unresolved issue from the start. Emperor Frederick II took the cross on his imperial coronation in 1215, but announced he was delaying his departure until 1219. In the event, he never joined the crusade. The leadership role that would have certainly been his on the grounds of the prestige of his title was instead split between the papal legate, Pelagius, and the only other king on crusade (Hugh of Cyprus having died in 1218 and Andrew II of Hungary having returned home), the king of Jerusalem, John of Brienne. They represented not only different approaches to crusading but also different constituencies. Whereas John and his barons were naturally keen to accept the offer that would see the return of the full kingdom of Jerusalem, the legate and many of the Western crusaders did not think that the recovery of the holy city could be accepted on such terms. There were other considerations. To abandon the conquest of Damietta was to give up the wealth of this great city and the possibility of acquiring more. If al-Kamil was so scared by the crusaders' strength that he was prepared to give this up, why not push him farther? Damietta was sure to fall to them anyway, and if they pushed down the Nile to Cairo they could surely extract even better terms. Finally, both the Hospitallers and the Templars advised against accepting the return of Jerusalem without the Transjordan castles: they were the hinge on which the defence of the holy city hung, and without them it would be likely to fall again.

The offer was refused, and the crusade stagnated in Damietta. The staggered effect of the separate armies' arrival and departure meant that some crusaders returned home after the city fell, and a period of recovery was needed until reinforcements arrived. This meant that momentum was lost, and an eyewitness to events, James of Vitry, testified to the difficulty of keeping the crusaders focused on the task at hand. Another factor was the topography of the Nile delta. The annual flooding of the delta that guaranteed its fertility – Egypt was the gift of the Nile, said an ancient proverb – also rendered it impassable to armies during the period of the floods, usually about three months during the summer. Therefore, if no advance were made before June, it could not be attempted again until the autumn. In the event, uncertainty about the arrival date of Emperor Frederick kept the crusaders penned up in Damietta until May 1221, when it finally became apparent that although he had sent a force of five hundred knights, he would not be taking part himself. The crusaders, egged on by Pelagius, decided to advance through the delta toward Cairo. It was a disastrous decision, because there was not enough time to accomplish the march and begin a siege before the floods. In fact, the crusaders were not as suicidal as it may now appear: the advance was probably an attempt to seize a newly built fortress halfway to Cairo in order to accomplish some result before the floods made such action impossible. But the Ayyubids used the canals that appeared during the flood season to surround the crusaders and cut them off from Damietta; they surrendered and terms were agreed for the withdrawal of the whole crusader army from Egypt at the end of June 1221.

Although al-Kamil was doubtless relieved at the departure of the crusaders, the Fifth Crusade had been a failure. Nothing of the conquest in Egypt remained, and by the time the crusaders left, rancour and mutual recriminations had taken the place of the apocalyptic enthusiasm of four years earlier. Another crusade organized and led by papal policy had ended in failure.

7

Unlikely success and glorious failure: royal crusades in the thirteenth century

Frederick II did not easily live down his failure to appear in person on the Fifth Crusade. By 1225, he had still not fulfilled the crusading vow he had taken ten years earlier. Pope Honorius III, in order to remind him of his interest in the fate of Jerusalem, arranged for him to marry the heiress to the kingdom of Jerusalem, Isabella II. The marriage was celebrated in 1225, and Frederick added the crown of Jerusalem to those of Sicily and the empire. Technically, he was consort rather than king in his own right, but the effect was the same. John of Brienne, the bride's father, had occupied the same position when he married Maria, the daughter of Isabella I and Conrad of Montferrat, in 1210. The royal house of Jerusalem had produced no male heir to the throne since the unfortunate Baldwin V in 1177, which meant that the future of the kingdom depended on marriage to members of the Western nobility. This had already been the case several times since 1129, but no Western husband imported into the kingdom had been as powerful as Frederick II.

The fact that Frederick was simply adding another crown to those he had already acquired through succession had serious implications for the kingdom of Jerusalem. He could not be expected, unlike Fulk V of Anjou in 1131, Guy of Lusignan in 1180, or John of Brienne in 1210, to forsake Western interests and devote himself exclusively to the fortunes of his new kingdom. But he did take his responsibilities seriously enough to oust Isabella's father, John of Brienne, from his seat on the throne. This not only contravened the undertakings given to John when he married Maria in 1210 that he would be king for life, but also broke with precedent: previous consorts of heiresses to the throne had been content to wait until the sitting ruler died. Frederick's impatience to act as king can also be seen in the unorthodox approach to the preparations for his crusade. He could now delay no longer and agreed to go to the East in August 1227 with a thousand knights and for at least two years. But at the same time he opened negotiations with al-Kamil, sultan of Egypt, who since the end of the Fifth Crusade had quarrelled with his brother al-Muazzam in Damascus. Frederick got al-Kamil to agree to restore Jerusalem and the full extent of the old kingdom of Jerusalem if he would help him deal with al-Muazzam, who as ruler in Damascus occupied the city of Jerusalem.

There was nothing new in a king of Jerusalem negotiating in this way with neighbouring Muslim powers; in fact, a policy of divide and rule was the best way for the kingdom to deal with the fact that, for the first time since 1174, southern Syria and Egypt were not in the hands of the same ruler. But it was certainly unusual for a crusade leader to be knee-deep in such machinations before even setting out for the East, and it was to have important consequences.

There is something inescapably farcical about Frederick's crusade. His army duly set out from Brindisi in August, but it was smaller than anticipated because an outbreak of disease had struck while the army was encamped and waiting for departure. Frederick himself had to turn back to port because he was too ill to continue. Earlier in the year 1227, a new pope, Gregory IX, had succeeded Honorius III. Gregory seems to have distrusted the emperor's motives from the start and interpreted his actions as a breach of the agreement to set out on crusade. He excommunicated Frederick, doubtless expecting the emperor to beg for pardon, so that he could extract concessions from him relating to his rule in Sicily. Frederick did no such thing, but finally set out in May 1228 with a much smaller force. Gregory's response was to excommunicate him again on the grounds that an excommunicate cannot go on crusade, but Frederick seems to have ignored this. The total number of troops at his disposal once the second contingent had met the original army was probably around 10,000, but Frederick was in no hurry to use the army. In any case, in November 1227, while Frederick was languishing in Sicily, al-Muazzam died, and al-Kamil lost no time in taking Jerusalem, thus rendering Frederick's strategy useless.

Before going to the Holy Land to see what could be done to salvage the crusade, Frederick turned his attention to Cyprus. This peaceful former province of the Byzantine Empire had been a godsend to the Franks of the kingdom of Jerusalem. Its conquest by Richard I in 1191 was followed by the settlement of large numbers of barons who were given fiefs there by the Lusignans. Richard used the conquest as a way of compensating Guy of Lusignan for the loss of the throne of Jerusalem in 1192, and when Guy died in 1194, it passed to his brother Aimery. Aimery's marriage to Isabella I in 1197 – her fourth marriage, after enforced divorce, murder and accidental death had removed her first three husbands – temporarily united the island with the kingdom of Jerusalem. Although this was a temporary union of royal persons rather than a constitutional merger of the two kingdoms, it provided the higher baronage with marriage opportunities that resulted, within a generation, in a situation very like that in England and Normandy after the Norman Conquest, in which the aristocracy occupied lands on both sides of the English Channel. But although the crown may have rested on a Lusignan

CYPRUS

Richard I conquered the island of Cyprus from the Byzantine prince Isaac Komnenos in 1191, under circumstances that could scarcely have been foreseen as part of the crusade. Isaac, a cousin of Emperor Andronikos Komnenos, had seized the island, a province of the Byzantine Empire, after the Komnenos dynasty was displaced in a *coup d'état* in 1185. In April 1191, while sailing from Sicily to the Holy Land, some of Richard's ships became separated from the rest of the crusading fleet during a storm, including the one carrying his sister Joanna and his fiancée, Berengaria of Navarre. The ship had found harbour in Limassol, on the south coast of Cyprus, but Isaac – who had a treaty with Saladin – kept them in harbour as his prisoners. When Richard arrived at Limassol, he forced an immediate landing, took the town by storm and, under cover of darkness, surrounded Isaac's camp, about five miles away. Isaac escaped, but his hold over the island's landowners was weakening, and he retreated to the mountainous north, where he hoped that the castles of Buffavento and St Hilarion would shield him from Richard. By now Richard seems to have decided that the conquest of the island would be strategically and financially beneficial, and when he took the fortified town of Kyrenia, on the northern coast, Isaac surrendered. Richard sold Cyprus to the Templars, but it was soon passed on to Guy of Lusignan, and after his death to his brother Aimery, who ruled it as a kingdom from 1194. The Lusignan dynasty continued to rule over the island in prosperity and relative peace until the fifteenth century, when it was acquired by Venice. It fell to the Ottomans in 1570.

head, the title to Cyprus was owned by the emperor, having been transferred in 1194 as part of the price of Richard's release by Emperor Henry VI. Frederick II was therefore perfectly entitled to inspect conditions in Cyprus and to deploy its resources as he saw fit in the governance of the kingdom of Jerusalem. This was especially so since in 1228 Cyprus was under a regency. Aimery and Isabella's son Hugh had died in 1218 and his widow, Alice of Champagne, had entrusted the government of the island to John of Ibelin, a prominent landowner of both kingdoms. Frederick suspected John of having embezzled funds from the royal treasury and took steps to humiliate and punish him. He was probably correct in his suspicions, but the Frankish barons of Cyprus and Jerusalem could not approve of the way he treated one of their number. Frederick tried to strip him of his lordship of Beirut, which was a fief of the kingdom of Jerusalem. John and most of his fellow barons lost no time in pointing out to Frederick that he could not constitutionally do this, since the two kingdoms were separate and a man could not be punished for misdemeanours in one by a penalty that applied to his property in the other. This degree of legalistic preciseness infuriated Frederick, but other than keeping John as his hostage when he moved across to Acre he could do little about it. In fact, his own position in the kingdom of Jerusalem was far from secure. His wife Isabella II had died early in 1228, and this left Frederick in no less vulnerable a position than his own father-in-law John of Brienne, whom he had stripped of authority in 1225. If anything, Frederick's position was worse, since, unlike John, he had never been crowned king of Jerusalem. The barons therefore regarded him as no more than regent on behalf of his infant son Conrad IV.

It must have been frustrating for the man who was in principle the most powerful figure in the Christian world to see his authority flouted by the barons of a tiny and weak state perched precariously on the fringes of Christendom. Perhaps their attitude would have been different had they thought Frederick was likely to do anything to improve their position. But his crusade had been planned as an alliance with al-Kamil before setting out; some of his troops had already gone home, and there seems to have been no Plan B. The best that he could do was to present a show of force and to try to persuade al-Kamil to keep his side of the bargain, even though he no longer needed Frederick's military help. Frederick certainly had no intention of risking war with al-Kamil by trying to take Jerusalem by force. For one thing, his army was not large enough; for another, he had other matters in the West that already demanded his attention. He was lucky that al-Kamil found the presence of a potentially hostile army in the Holy Land awkward at a time when he himself wanted to take the war to al-Muazzam's heir in Damascus. Al-Kamil, not wanting Frederick's army in the Holy Land, agreed to buy him off with the return of the city of Jerusalem. Even a small crusading force might prove dangerous, especially since, as al-Kamil realized, Frederick could not return to the West without having tried to gain anything for Christendom. The conditions of return were that the city's defensive walls would be destroyed and the Islamic holy sites of the al-Aqsa mosque and Dome of the Rock would remain in Muslim hands. As Frederick boasted in a letter to King Henry III of England, he had in fact achieved more than the return of the holy city: Bethlehem and other parts of Judaea, Nazareth and parts of the Galilee, and half of Sidon were also restored to the kingdom, and a truce was concluded for another ten years and ten months.

To his surprise, nobody seemed impressed or even pleased by the outcome of his expedition. Frederick sealed the terms of the treaty with al-Kamil by holding a ceremonial crown-wearing in the Church of the Holy Sepulchre in Jerusalem. But he could not hear Mass there, because Patriarch Gerold had, on the instructions of Gregory IX, placed the holy city under an interdict. This meant that no sacraments could be dispensed, no Masses could be heard, and no one could be baptized, given the last rites or buried in consecrated ground. It was an extraordinary situation, and one that shows how far Frederick had failed to win over either the pope or the Latin Church in the East. In fact, he seemed instead to flaunt his relationship with the Ayyubids. The Arab chronicler Sibt Ibn al-Jauzi tells the story of Frederick castigating the imam of the al–Aqsa mosque for forbidding the call of the muezzin out of respect for the Christian emperor while he was in Jerusalem. Frederick protested that as a Sicilian he was quite accustomed to hearing the call and that he had looked forward to hearing it in Jerusalem. The emperor, al-Jauzi concluded, was an atheist.

Other local constituencies were also unimpressed by Frederick. Although he had regained the holy city, he had left it defenceless by agreeing to the terms that did not permit rebuilding its walls. The lands he had secured were not, as they doubtless anticipated, returned to the baronial families who had held them before 1187, but given instead to the Teutonic Knights, the German Military Order formed during the Third Crusade and patronized by Frederick. Moreover, Frederick did nothing to resolve the constitutional crisis that he had caused by depriving the crowned king, John of Brienne, of his authority. The High Court of the kingdom's barons simply refused to accept that Frederick was in fact king of Jerusalem. So low had the emperor's reputation sunk that when he left the Holy Land in 1229, he was pelted with offal by the market stallholders in Acre.

Frederick never again had the opportunity to go to the East, but he did not relinquish his claims to governance of the kingdom of Jerusalem. Throughout the 1230s, the baronage was split between allegiance to his representatives, particularly the Italian Riccardo Filangieri, and to the principle of baronial near-autonomy championed by the Ibelins and their allies. The barons were in no position to do anything to safeguard the gains made by the treaty of 1229, but as early as 1234 Gregory IX was already preparing a fresh expedition for this purpose. In the event, the Barons' Crusade, as it is known, took on an unusual character. Essentially it was an Anglo-French expedition led by some of the great barons of the Capetian and Angevin kingdoms. Recruitment, however, was partly determined by the political framework of the 1230s in both kingdoms. Louis IX of France and Henry III of England had both come to the throne as minors and therefore had to undergo regencies before they could assume personal rule. In the 1230s both suffered challenges to their authority. Louis had overcome these by 1236, but in order to preserve the peace he exiled one of the leading troublemakers, Thibaut IV, count of Champagne, for seven years; another, Peter, duke of Brittany, promised to take the cross and go to the Holy Land for five years. Several others joined them, including the duke of Burgundy and the count of Mâcon. They were encouraged and even financially supported by the crown. The English contingent was recruited and organized later than the French, so the crusade was staggered and had a dual character. It was led by Richard, earl of Cornwall, Henry III's brother, and included other barons who saw it as an opportunity to win back favour with the crown after the political crisis of Henry's minority.

By 1239, when the French crusaders left, al-Kamil had died and Egypt and Damascus were once again under separate control. Moreover, the Ayyubid dynasty was breaking up in the face of both succession disputes and the threat of a new power in the Near East, the Khwarazmian Turks. Although neither the French nor English crusaders won a military victory, Thibaut's treaties of 1240 with both the sultans of Egypt and Damascus, and Richard's successful negotiations with Ayyub of Egypt, which resulted in the Muslim evacuation of Jerusalem, were productive for the kingdom of Jerusalem. Frederick, still regarding himself as ruler of the kingdom, endorsed Richard's diplomacy in the East by sending an embassy to Egypt in 1242–3 to confirm his arrangements. At this time, the kingdom's territory stood at its greatest territorial extent since 1187.

Both Frederick's crusade and the Barons' Crusade ten years later showed that the fate of the Holy Land could be helped by small-scale expeditions whose intent was to consolidate and maintain pressure on local rulers, as well as by large-scale crusades. Spectacular military action, however, was irresistible to some crusaders. In December 1244, Louis IX, having secured his kingdom, took the cross. Local circumstances and the changing political climate in the East shed some light on his decision, but ultimately this was a highly personal crusade. Although English knights and Franks from Greece took part, along with barons from the kingdoms of Jerusalem and Cyprus, and although he tried to interest the king of Norway in joining him, Louis' crusade was overwhelmingly a French royal expedition. The timing is intriguing. In August 1244, Jerusalem was overrun by the Khwarazmians, who had been called in by Ayyub, sultan of Egypt, as allies against his rivals. The viciousness of their attack, in which the Greek Orthodox patriarch and the entire community of Armenian monks in Jerusalem were killed, was on a scale not seen in the city since the crusaders' arrival in 1099. The Franks of the kingdom of Jerusalem joined forces with Ayyub's rivals, principally Ismail, sultan of Damascus. The Khwarazmians were too powerful for the alliance, and at the Battle of La Forbie, near Gaza, on 17 October, they crushed the Franks and Damascenes. It was, in terms of loss of manpower, a worse disaster for the Franks than Hattin. About 1,100 of the 2,000 or so Frankish knights were from the three main Military Orders: of these, only 69 survived. In all, the total losses were reported by the patriarch of Jerusalem as 16,000 men. The defeat did not mean the end of the kingdom of Jerusalem, but it would not be far-fetched to see it as the beginning of that eventual end.

Louis' commitment to the crusade was probably an instinctive and emotional response to the news that Jerusalem had been violently re-occupied by a Muslim force. He was a few weeks in advance of Pope Innocent IV's public appeal for a crusade, launched at the Council of Lyons in January 1245. Louis had already signalled his devotion to the Holy Land by buying from the bankrupt Latin emperor of Constantinople the relic of the crown of thorns in 1239, and building that glorious Gothic gem, the Sainte-Chapelle church in Paris, to house it. Louis began recruiting amongst his barons in 1245, but it was not until three years later that he was ready to leave for the East. The preparations were the most painstaking and far-reaching of any crusade up to that point. French towns and French clergy were taxed heavily, and Louis even bought land to build a new port at Aigues-Mortes on the south coast. His army assembled at Cyprus from September 1248 and settled in for the autumn and winter. This gave time for speculation and approaches from various interested parties. Clearly the arrival of such a powerful army was of interest to rulers such as the Latin emperor of Constantinople, Prince Bohemond V of Antioch, and the Seljuq sultan in Asia Minor; even the Mongols sent an envoy to Louis. The arrival of non-Christian delegations shows how deeply crusading, and the regular presence of Western Christian armies, had penetrated under the skin of local politics.

It was not until May 1249 that Louis was finally ready to begin the attack. His army numbered up to 2,800 mounted knights, 5,000 crossbowmen and about 15,000 foot soldiers – considerably more than any crusading force since the Fifth Crusade. Like the leaders of that ill-fated expedition, Louis determined from the outset to attack Egypt. Both politically and strategically, this made good sense. The Ayyubid regime was known to be failing, and Louis doubtlessly thought he could take advantage of a power vacuum. Moreover, the strategy of conquering Egypt in order to gain a stranglehold over the Holy Land was as valid in 1249 as it had been thirty years earlier. As long ago as 1192, the Third Crusade had exposed the flaw in the strategy of a direct assault on Jerusalem. Unless a crusading army could engage and inflict a decisive defeat on those who controlled the Holy Land, any success on crusade would be only temporary, for even if Jerusalem were captured, it could easily be recovered once the crusade had left for the West. The only way to ensure that the force so expensively and painstakingly assembled was not dissipated was to risk it in battle, and this meant, in the first place, identifying and engaging the enemy. A cautious defending commander could simply avoid giving battle and, as Saladin had done in 1192, outlast the crusade.

The initial attack on Egypt could not have gone better. The Egyptians abandoned Damietta after only the most cursory resistance, and the city was secured early in June 1249. This meant that Louis was further ahead of schedule than he had predicted. Time that might have been expected to have been spent in the siege of Damietta could in fact be used to settle French royal rule in the city. By the autumn, Louis had restored the cathedral founded in 1220 by the fifth crusaders and staffed it with a French bishop and clergy. He had also begun to recruit French settlers – but had quarrelled with the crusaders from the kingdom of Jerusalem, who considered his annexation of Damietta to the French crown to be contrary to crusading custom. The decision that now had to be made was whether to press on down the Nile towards Cairo or to secure the conquest of Alexandria first. The bolder choice, a march down the Nile, prevailed. As the king's brother, Robert of Artois, famously observed, it was better to crush the head of the serpent than its tail. This decision seemed to have been vindicated when news came of the death of Sultan Ayyub just days after the army had set out on its march south. The first obstacle faced by the army was the fortress at Mansurah, but in order to take it the crusaders had to cross the Nile. Although Louis had provided for this eventuality by bringing engineers to construct a causeway, they had not foreseen that the Egyptians would be able to cut away earth at the opposite bank to widen the channel. Eventually Louis abandoned the attempt in favour of fording the river further downstream where it was shallower. This crossing point, however, was narrow enough to slow down the army. Their troubles were compounded by the insistence of Robert of Artois on leading the vanguard ahead of the Templars – who, by tradition, held that honour – in an assault on the fortress. Robert's knights overran the Egyptian camp, but in the streets of Mansurah they were cut to pieces by the Egyptian Mamluks. Robert himself, along with William Longsword and many of the English knights, was killed. All this had happened while much of the crusading army, including the crossbowmen, was still on the opposite bank of the Nile. Louis had no option but to halt the march to Cairo. The battle for Mansurah might justifiably be called a draw rather than a defeat, but the effect was that the momentum of the crusade was halted. How much of the blame should be levelled at Robert of Artois – or, indeed, at Louis himself for failing to control his younger brother – is debatable. Medieval cavalry forces, once committed to combat, were very difficult to control, but the results of battles often rested on taking the initiative at the right time, and had Robert's gamble succeeded, the crusaders would have been in a remarkably strong position.

Although the Battle of Mansurah was a huge disappointment, Louis still held a trump card in his possession: Damietta. As in 1219, its return could be negotiated for Jerusalem. But while negotiations were underway, the Egyptians had cut the communications with Damietta by launching galleys upstream on the Nile. In April 1250, Louis, himself ill from dysentery, gave the order to retreat to Damietta. Before the army reached the safety of the city, and in circumstances of some confusion among the crusaders, they were forced by illness and shortage of food to surrender. They were fortunate that Louis' wife, Margaret, who was heavily pregnant, had the fortitude to keep control of the garrison at Damietta. As it turned out, Frankish possession of the city was needed not, as it had once been hoped, to negotiate the return of Jerusalem, but to ransom King Louis and his army. The sum set was a massive 400,000 pounds of silver, but for the first instalment Louis had to rely on the Templars.

Until he had paid the whole amount, Frankish prisoners had to languish in Egypt, and although he had initially planned to leave the Latin East to its fate after the disappointments of the crusade, Louis was persuaded to remain in Acre until the whole army had been ransomed. This gave a new complexion to the whole crusade, and in the event Louis stayed in the kingdom of

Jerusalem until 1254. He spent much of his time reconstructing fortifications, but he also became involved in the shifting sands of regional politics. After his withdrawal from Damietta, Egypt had fallen into the hands of the Mamluks, the slave-soldiers of the Ayyubid regime. He toyed with the idea of an alliance with an-Nasir, the sultan of Aleppo and conqueror of Damascus, against the Mamluks, but feared reprisals against those of his army still in captivity in Egypt. In the end, he was able to profit from Damascus–Mamluk conflicts and consolidate the position of the kingdom of Jerusalem. At one point it looked as though he might still renegotiate the return of Jerusalem by playing a role similar to that of Frederick II in 1229, but he had to content himself with safeguarding the kingdom by means of treaties. He also provided kingship for a kingdom that not only had no king, but had been beset by political squabbles over governance. In fact, Frederick II's son, Conrad IV, the only king recognized by the barons of the kingdom, died without heirs in May 1254, leaving a constitutional vacancy in the kingdom.

Louis did not abandon the cause of Jerusalem even after returning to France. He left behind a hundred knights to be maintained out of royal funds, and this arrangement, which was continued by his successors, gave the French crown permanent representation in the kingdom of Jerusalem until 1291. But equally important to his kingship was the experience of having led a crusade to the East. Although he had failed to restore Jerusalem after its loss in 1244, or to do much for the kingdom in material terms, his own reputation as a crusading king made him a force to be reckoned with at home. Louis' biographer, the Champenois knight Jean de Joinville, recalled more than fifty years after the crusade something that the king had remarked to him as he sailed away from Damietta, still weak from the dysentery he had suffered in Egypt. The humiliation of sickness and defeat, he confided, was in one way welcome, because it enabled him to understand more clearly the sufferings of Christ. Doubtless there was a good deal of pious rhetoric in this, but it does reveal something of the king's mindset. For Louis as a Christian king, the crusade was an obligation. Taking part in the struggle against the Muslim world was what mattered above all.

8

The loss of the Holy Land

Between Louis IX's glorious failure and the fall of the kingdom of Jerusalem in 1291, the near-eastern world changed out of all recognition. The first signs of such a dramatic change were apparent for Louis himself to see, but he cannot be blamed for not having understood their significance. While he was acting as surrogate ruler in Jerusalem after his defeat in Egypt, the ambassadors he had sent to the Great Khan of the Mongols two years previously returned from the unimaginably distant lands far to the east beyond the Islamic world. These were lands that few Europeans had seen in the middle of the thirteenth century, though there were various theories about who lived there and what they were like. Since the 1140s, Europeans had been convinced that a powerful Christian king ruled over an indeterminate stretch of Asia. This was based on what was in fact a reality: namely, that many of the nomadic Mongols had been converted to Christianity by the Church of the East. Contacts between the West and the Church of the East, which had been separated from both Latin and Greek Christianity since the fifth century and was predominantly based in Iraq, were sporadic, but periodically rumours of the deeds of Mongol khans reflected actual events in Central and East Asia.

By the 1240s, they were more than rumours. Under the leadership of Genghis Khan – who was not one of those who had converted to Christianity – the Mongols had become apparently invincible as they cut swathes westward across Asia. When the answer to

Louis' embassy finally came, it was chilling in its self-confidence and disregard for the established European order. The regent for the Great Khan, Oghul-Qaimish, declared that the Mongols could not enter into an alliance of friendship with Louis, but that they would graciously accept his homage and in the capacity of overlords extend their protection over the French king. French diplomatic approaches went no further, but the Mongols continued to advance. In 1258 they were at the gates of Baghdad. Europeans must have heard in amazement and disbelief the news of the sack of the capital of the Abbasid caliphate, the slaughter of its inhabitants and the destruction of its mosques and palaces. Damascus fell shortly afterwards, and although the Mongols provided the main muscle, Bohemond VI of Antioch, by agreeing to the terms that Louis IX had refused, found himself entering in triumph the city that crusaders had failed to conquer by themselves. It must have seemed as though the Islamic world was close to collapse.

It was to be a false dawn. In 1260, the Franks of the Crusader States could only stand by and watch as the Mongols and the 'lion of Egypt', the Mamluk leader Baibars, clashed at Ain Jalut, in Galilee. It was to prove the first military reverse that the Mongols had experienced, and it secured the future of the Mamluk regime. The Mongols remained a potent presence and periodically over the next forty years provided tantalizing glimpses of what might have been achievable if they had been able to work effectively with Western crusaders. Embassies to Edward I in England in the 1280s, and temporary alliances in the Near East with Armenia and Antioch, promised joint action against the Mamluks. But the Mongols had spread themselves thinly, and the Near East was only one of their theatres of operation. Even with their ferocity and military skill in the field, co-ordination with Western forces was needed if they were to dominate a settled urban landscape, and this was never achieved.

Louis IX's expedition to Egypt was to be the last large-scale 'traditional' crusade to the East for a hundred and fifty years. In the

Figure 7 Louis IX sets sail for the crusade of 1270. (Source: From a fourteenth-century manuscript of the *Chroniques de France*, British Library Royal MS 16 G.VI, f.437v.)

1260s and 1270s papal policy with regard to crusading changed. For one thing, with the exception of Gregory X (1271–6), no pope before 1290 showed much interest in the Holy Land or in launching a new crusade. But even Gregory X himself, while committed to crusading, advocated a more nuanced policy than the traditional 'general passage', as it was known to contemporaries, in which large armies were amassed from across Christian Europe for a single campaign. Instead, kings were encouraged to follow the policy of Louis IX himself after 1254 and make commitments to maintain bodies of knights in the Crusader States for indefinite periods to aid in their defence. This is not to say that no new crusades were planned or launched, but the fate of the crusade of 1270 did not inspire further confidence in the traditional format.

Louis IX's second crusading venture proved disastrous. It was intended as a pan-European expedition and featured an English army led by the heir to the throne, Edward, an Aragonese–Catalan fleet dispatched by James I, and an army provided by Louis' younger brother Charles of Anjou, king of Sicily. But the crusade fractured in the heat and dust of Tunis in the summer of 1270. The diversion to North Africa was supposed to be a preliminary sideshow before all the forces met in the East, but Louis' siege of Tunis failed, he himself died, and Charles, arriving late, abandoned the expedition. The Aragonese–Catalan fleet was dispersed by storms, and Edward was left with a force too small to accomplish anything in the kingdom of Jerusalem.

Tedaldo Visconti was one of the clergy accompanying Edward when he heard, late in 1271, that he had been elected pope. As Gregory X, he convened the Second Council of Lyons in 1274 to find a solution to the problem of launching a successful crusade. Although his own death in 1276 put an end to whatever momentum it might have had, Gregory's proposed crusade marked the first papal attempt since Innocent III to consider the problems rationally. A series of written reflections on crusading, known by historians as 'recovery treatises', was initiated by the Council. Dozens were written between the 1270s and 1320s by a wide variety of people – the Armenian prince Hethoum II; the grand master of the Hospitallers, Fulk of Villaret; a prominent Venetian merchant, Mario Sanudo; missionaries, such as the Dominicans William Adam and William of Tripoli, and the Franciscan Fidenzo of Padua; and civil servants, such as the French bureaucrat Pierre Dubois. Taken together, they show a strikingly penetrative analysis of the difficulties of crusading: the problems of military co-ordination and logistics; the challenge of raising sufficient funds and ensuring they were spent wisely and by the right people; the need for an economic as well as a military strategy in the East; the fragmented nature of European as well as Levantine Christian society. Above all, perhaps, they reveal a crisis of confidence in crusading. This is not to say that the ideal was less popular than it had been fifty or a hundred years earlier; rather, that the premises on which crusading had been built in the first place were shifting.

Victory over the Mongols in 1260 had handed the Mamluks the initiative in what now became a struggle to obliterate the Crusader States entirely. Whereas Saladin's Ayyubid successors had been prepared to live and let live, Baibars and the Mamluk regime, like Saladin himself, saw the very existence of the Crusader States as an affront to Islam. The thirty years after Ain Jalut saw the gradual dismemberment of the Crusader States. In 1265, Baibars launched a sweeping attack on the kingdom of Jerusalem, capturing Caesarea, and effectively cutting the coastal strip controlled by the Christians in two. Further campaigns ate away at the kingdom still further, until, by Baibars' death in 1277, it was reduced to a few coastal cities and the enclaves around them. The failure of the royal line did not help matters. After the death of Emperor Frederick II's heir, Conrad IV, in 1254 and his son, Conradin, in 1266 – neither of whom had even been to the East – there was no clear succession to the throne. Neither of the disputing claimants, Hugh III of Cyprus and his aunt Maria of Antioch, was able to mobilize sufficient military support to secure it – nor indeed to do anything to stem the tide of military defeats at the hands of the Mamluks. The one figure who had the resources, the authority and the stature to defend the kingdom of Jerusalem was Charles of Anjou, king of Sicily. In a moment of striking constitutional significance, he bought out Maria of Antioch's claim to the throne in 1277. Although Pope Gregory X was reluctant to recognize the legitimacy of his title, he encouraged Charles to support the kingdom through regular subsidies of military supplies and money to the Military Orders. Perhaps Charles might have made a difference had he been able to take an army to the East, but in 1282 the outbreak of revolt against Angevin rule on the island of Sicily – the so-called 'Sicilian

Vespers' – effectively put an end to any such hopes. The revolt, in which the Greek-speaking population of Sicily was secretly encouraged by the Byzantine Emperor Michael VIII, also brought the Aragonese kingdom, conquerors of the Balearic Islands, into the central Mediterranean.

Not until 1285 did the kingdom of Jerusalem finally have an undisputed king, with the accession of Henry II of Cyprus. While the kingdom of Jerusalem had suffered a steady decline in its fortunes since the mid-thirteenth century, Cyprus thrived. After Frederick II's failure between 1228 and 1232 to exercise direct control over what was nominally his subject territory, the Lusignans ruled in relative security over a prosperous and peaceful island. Most of the major landowners were barons from the old kingdom of Jerusalem who had originally been given lands on the island by Aimery or his successors. Although they retained their titles from the kingdom, their profits and such power as they had came mostly from Cyprus. One wonders just how committed most of them were to a continuing investment in the kingdom of Jerusalem.

The fall of Antioch in 1268 ended Frankish rule in north Syria, and by 1289, when Tripoli fell, only Acre, Tyre and a small hinterland remained. Although the West responded to the final threat to Acre in 1291, such military aid as arrived was too little and too late. After a desperate siege in which as many Christian inhabitants as possible were evacuated, the city, and with it the kingdom of Jerusalem, fell in May 1291, just short of two hundred years after the successful conclusion of the First Crusade. A contemporary poem mourning the fall of Acre blamed the inactivity and idleness of kings, pope and people in the West, but although the immediate reaction was one of shock, it proved impossible to organize a crusade of recovery. The contrast with 1187 is instructive: then, papal pressure forced the kings of England and France to shelve their quarrels in order to save Jerusalem; a hundred years later, England and France were still in a state of hostilities, but had other priorities than the Holy Land. Momentum was everything, and no major relief expedition was ever launched.

Why did Europeans in 1291 fail so signally to leap to the defence of the Christian Holy Land? One answer is that the conditions facing them were far more difficult than ever before. The Christian victory on the First Crusade and the establishment of the Crusader States would never have been possible had the Islamic world not been undergoing a period of political disarray; a period that did not end until Saladin's rise to power. Moreover, after the Ayyubid dynasty collapsed in 1250, the Mamluks were able to assume power in Egypt and Syria with hardly any disruption. In contrast, thirteenth-century Europe did not offer the same conditions for crusading that had been present at the end of the eleventh century. Both Church and kingdoms were more centralized and more effective in exercising power than their predecessors had been, but paradoxically this did not lead to more effective crusading. As late as 1217, crusaders could be recruited by direct papal appeal, and lordship was still an important factor in recruitment, as it had been in 1095. The Fifth Crusade was the last major expedition in which overall leadership and organization was not provided by a king. From the middle of the thirteenth century onward, it was kings, or at any rate the heads of states, who took on responsibility for organizing crusades. The reason for this was precisely the increased centralization of royal power. Kings such as Edward I were increasingly unwilling to allow resources, in the form of either knights or money, to leave their kingdoms without royal authority. Ties of lordship, with their obligations on both barons and kings, were defined more closely than ever before. Above all, the ways in which armies were raised was very different from the eleventh and twelfth centuries. Contractual terms of pay were a standard form of recruitment by Edward I's reign, where even fifty years earlier his father had been able to raise armies by calling on traditional obligations of service. Louis IX's first crusade was probably the last in which knights took the cross purely of their own volition and paid – or tried to pay – their own way.

Moreover, the system devised by the papacy under Innocent III for financing crusades by now relied on the functions of royal governments to make it work successfully. Innocent's idea, stimulated by the failure of financial arrangements on the Fourth Crusade, was to pay for crusading by imposing an income tax on the clergy of Christendom. Since the clergy were supported by tithes paid by the laity, this was effectively a form of indirect taxation on Christian Europe. It relied, of course, on how efficiently bishops collected the tax and passed it on to the papacy – and ultimately, on how effectively the money was spent by the pope. In principle, it was probably as good a system as could have been devised in the conditions of the early thirteenth century, but by the end of the century those conditions no longer applied. Popes whose priorities lay elsewhere than the Holy Land could use the money for any other purpose, which risked the credibility of the tax in the eyes of the laity. Kings became increasingly unwilling to allow the coin of their subjects to swell the coffers of the pope; by the 1290s, both Philip IV of France and Edward I of England were denying that popes had any authority to levy taxes on their clerical subjects. In such circumstances, crusading tithes became difficult for the Church to collect. Papal commissioners might be sent to do the collecting, but there was no guarantee they would come away with any money. In 1245, a papal legate was thrown bodily out of Oxford by the students and townspeople when he tried to collect a crusading tithe for purposes that seemed dubious at best. By the last quarter of the thirteenth century, therefore, popes had delegated the task of collecting tithes for crusading to royal governments. Kings who took the cross were granted a tithe in the form of a certain percentage of clerical incomes for a given number of years. Such tithes were far more likely to be collected than when the system relied on the bishops or papal commissioners. But just as popes might spend the money on more immediate projects, so might kings. When Charles IV became king of France in 1322, Pope John XXII immediately wrote to him reminding him that his brother Philip V (1316–22), whose throne he had inherited, had been granted a tithe in order to lead a crusade, and that the responsibility for the crusade now fell on Charles himself. The new king found that the tithe had indeed been collected – and already spent on something completely different and more urgent.

The shock of the fall of Acre was felt throughout Europe, and can be traced in scores of contemporary laments, poems, songs and bitter invectives against those who were considered to have failed in their duty of defending Jerusalem. Christians of Western origin living in the Crusader States fled, if they were able, to Cyprus, whose population must have increased noticeably in the early fourteenth century. Those who could not flee in time, or could not afford passage to Cyprus, became prisoners of the Mamluks. A contemporary account of the lines of Christian families tramping into a distant captivity still has power to move by its pathos. The native Arabic-speaking Christians remained as they had always done, to live once more under Islamic rule. As far as they were able, Latin religious communities resettled in Cyprus or further afield. Many had properties in the West on which they could live. The Military Orders suffered an immediate loss of credibility as a result of their failure to defend Acre successfully. The Hospitallers were able to regroup, initially on Cyprus, but subsequently on the island of Rhodes, which became part of the frontline in the defence of the Aegean against the Ottomans. Their role in nursing the sick and wounded gave them a viable reason for continuing to call upon the patronage and support of Christendom. The Templars, however, were unable to find a new role after the fall of Acre. Their wealth and perceived arrogance made them an obvious target, and Philip IV of France began proceedings against the Order with the compliance of a French pope, Clement V. The charges against them, ranging from necromancy to homosexuality, were mostly fabricated, but from the outside the Order must indeed have seemed secretive, exclusive and complacent. Although the cruelty of the judicial executions of the grand master, Jacques de Molay, and other Templars moved many to pity, they found few defenders.

Neither popes nor kings forgot crusading, but once the kingdom of Jerusalem had ceased to exist, strategic priorities changed. Given that, unlike in 1187, there was no longer any Western Christian presence on the Asian mainland, a new crusade would be a question not of reinforcing a struggling polity but of launching an invasion comparable to the First Crusade and of carving out new territories. Such an enterprise was rendered more difficult by the Mamluks' destruction of the crusader cities they had taken along with their harbours. The immediate concern in the early years of the fourteenth century was the protection of the Christian powers still standing in the eastern Mediterranean: Cyprus and Cilician Armenia. Pope John XXII (1316–34) tried to establish a naval league to protect them, with the support of the king and queen of Naples and the Hospitallers, now based on Rhodes. Christian efforts, however, were outpaced by the changing face of the Near East itself. Protecting Christendom in the Mediterranean meant tracking any new threats, and this quickly came to entail a new set of imperatives from the recovery of the Holy Land. By the time the last major attempt to recover the kingdom of Jerusalem was being planned – Philip VI's proposed crusade of 1336, which never took place – it was already an anachronism.

Subsequent European efforts in the eastern Mediterranean would confront a new power – the Ottoman Turks. From the 1330s, the Ottomans, originally a steppe people from Central Asia, spread westward until, by the end of the century, they had swept through Asia Minor and stood at the gates of Europe. Constantinople lay at their mercy. The Byzantine Empire, though restored to its ancestral capital in 1261 with the collapse of the ill-fated Latin Empire, never recovered the status or power it had enjoyed in the twelfth century, let alone in days of earlier glory. Parts of Greece were still in the hands of Latin families, while most of the islands, including Crete, were Venetian; the advance of the Ottomans swallowed up Greek Asia Minor and, by the end of the fourteenth century, Thrace and much of the Balkans. The decisive Ottoman victory over the Serbian kingdom at Kosovo in 1389 was an alarming confirmation of the threat they now posed to central Europe. In a few outbursts of 'traditional' crusading fervour, some Europeans sought to remind their contemporaries that the Holy Land was still in Muslim hands. In the 1360s, King John of France seemed poised to send an expedition to Cyprus to join the Lusignan King Peter I in a new crusade, but he died before it could be launched, and although Peter's crusade did succeed in briefly capturing Alexandria in 1365, the momentum was not sustained. More typical of the direction of fourteenth-century crusading efforts was the disastrous Crusade of Nicopolis of 1396, in which a French–Burgundian force joined King Sigismund of Hungary in attacking the Ottoman fortress of Nicopolis on the Danube. The Ottomans sent a relieving army, and in the resulting clash the crusaders, largely because they ignored Hungarian advice on how to fight the Turks, were heavily defeated. Any further prospects of a royal Anglo-French crusade to save Constantinople were doomed, and even though the Byzantine Emperor Manuel II roused plenty of sympathy when he toured European courts in 1400–1, no further help was forthcoming.

Coming as it did during a lull in the Hundred Years' War between England and France, this expedition might have served to revive Western royal interest in the eastern Mediterranean. Instead, leadership in crusading passed to the Burgundian ducal house, a state rich and powerful enough by *c.*1400 to assemble large armies, and with pretensions to quasi-imperial rule in the Low Countries and eastern France that might be well served by reviving crusading ideals. So thorough was the defeat at Nicopolis, however, that when an opportunity to strike against the Ottomans arose in 1402, it was missed. The rise of the brilliant central Asian warlord Tamerlane, who attacked the Ottomans from the east, might have opened up such an opportunity had the West been able to take advantage. Briefly it looked as though the Ottoman state might fracture, but by the time recovery was under way under Mehmet I (1413–21), England and France were at war again. The period of Ottoman reconstruction after the whirlwind of Tamerlane's conquests meant that Constantinople was safe for a time, but by the 1430s Mehmet's son Murad II (1421–51) was ready to advance into Europe again. This time, he exploited the death of Sigismund of Hungary in 1437 to invade Transylvania and Serbia. In 1441 and 1442, the governor of Transylvania, John Hunyadi, showed what could be done by defeating the Ottomans decisively in battle. Moreover, the papacy under Eugenius IV had tried to reanimate crusading interest by securing the union of Latin and Greek Churches at the Council of Florence (1439). In the early 1440s, unified European holy war against the Turks seemed as likely as at any time since 1291. As before, it was to prove a false hope.

The intention was to launch a co-ordinated attack by sea against Ottoman naval power in the Dardanelles at the same time as a Hungarian–Polish land assault in the Balkans. A preliminary Hungarian-led expedition in 1443 captured Sofia and Nish, but lacked naval support. Although the co-ordination seemed to be in place a year later, the Venetian fleet failed to stop Murad II from reinforcing his Balkan armies from across the Dardanelles, and when the Christian army reached Varna, on the Black Sea, they found themselves hopelessly outnumbered. King Wladyslaw of Hungary was killed in the fighting, and the crusade disintegrated. The reasons for the crusaders' defeat are far from obvious. The Ottomans themselves took the threat posed by Christian unity very seriously, and Murad's attempts to forestall the expedition by offering terms to the Hungarians undermined Wladyslaw's authority at home, making it difficult to raise an army of the size that was needed two years in succession. Following Varna, Constantinople was effectively doomed, and although its fall to Mehmet II in 1453 was accompanied by soul-searching and grief in the West, the formal end of the Roman Empire can have come as no surprise.

Although the Ottomans posed the greatest threat to Christendom and occupied the bulk of strategic thinking about holy war, the eastern Mediterranean and Balkans were only one theatre of crusading. It is striking that many of the French and Burgundian knights who took part at Nicopolis in 1396 were experienced crusaders, though none of their experience had been gained in fighting the Turks. Chaucer's knight, more or less a contemporary of the Nicopolis crusade, had been on crusade both in Spain and in the Baltic. It was in the latter arena especially that most crusaders gained their experience in the fourteenth century, and where holy war ideals were most regularly ingrained in the European knighthood.

Crusading in the Baltic began with an expedition by north German knights in 1147 against the pagan Wends of the Pomeranian coast. Piggy-backing on the Second Crusade, they sought and secured papal approval on the same terms as the expedition to the eastern Mediterranean on the grounds that they were simply applying the same principles of defending Christendom against non-Christians in their own backyard. This was effectively German colonial expansion into new territories, but it was given new impetus by the formation of the Teutonic Knights on the Third Crusade. Although the Knights continued to maintain their headquarters in the Holy Land, they diverted increasing resources to their presence in the Baltic. A German trading settlement and a new bishopric at Riga in the early thirteenth century gave the Knights and their compatriots such as the dreaded Sword Brothers the opportunity to present their activities as a defensive war. Sporadically throughout the thirteenth century and for much of the fourteenth, the Teutonic Knights posed as the bulwark of the faith against the enemies of Christendom. In truth, it was a dirty and increasingly territorial war, in which the Knights became effectively rulers of the state that would eventually transform itself in the sixteenth century into the duchy of Prussia. Nevertheless, it gave opportunities for knights from all over Europe to participate in a holy war. During the fourteenth century, when similar opportunities to take the cross against the Turks were limited, campaigning for a season with the Teutonic Knights became a popular option. One could spend a chivalric winter based at one of the Knights' castles such as Marienburg (Malbork, now in Poland), hunting and feasting, with a foray or two against the local Lithuanians to provide a badge of honour. But the Teutonic Knights were never particularly popular within the Church, and while knights could always be recruited, there was also criticism both of their methods and of the assumptions underlying their existence. The very legitimacy of their crusading activities came under scrutiny from the Church at the Council of Constance (1414–18). In a sense, they had crusaded themselves out of a job, since the conversion of the kings of Lithuania to Christianity rendered their arguments about the threats of pagan rulers to Christendom specious. Pope Martin V (1417–31) refused to grant approval for their war against Lithuania–Poland.

There were other opportunities throughout the thirteenth and fourteenth centuries for knights who were not overly concerned with the targets of holy war. At just around the time when the vocabulary of crusading was coming to have more precise implications in legal terms, from the 1190s onward, Innocent III saw how the spiritual benefits of holy war could be applied to a range of conflicts. In 1199 he hinted that those who supported papal political interests in Italy against the threat of the Hohenstaufen could be seen as crusaders, and in 1208 he preached a crusade against Count RaymondVI ofToulouse for harbouring heretics. The Albigensian Crusade (1209–29) became, in effect, a papally sponsored war of aggression waged by northern French barons against Provençal landowning society. In 1245, Innocent IV turned an existing struggle for the defence of the papal states in central Italy against Emperor Frederick II into a crusade, and enemies of the papacy in the messy fourteenth-century territorial conflicts in Italy might at any time have crusades launched against them. In principle, there was no difference in status between such wars and the campaigns for the defence or recovery of the Holy Land in the East. Whether contemporaries saw things in such relativist terms is not easy to gauge; presumably they were keen to benefit spiritually from taking the cross whenever such benefits were on offer from the papacy, but there is some evidence that knights did not always see an exact correlation. The Albigensian Crusade, for example, was unpopular in the Empire because it was seen to be diverting funds that might have benefited the Holy Land to regional interests in the West. Innocent IV's attempt to sell the kingdom of Sicily to Richard of Cornwall, younger brother of Henry III of England, was unpopular in England because it was seen as a blatant way of raising money from crusading tithes in support of the political interests of the papacy. Richard of Cornwall had led a crusading army to the Holy Land in 1239–41, and some of the English knights who had taken the cross with him resented the attempt by the papal legate to persuade them to transfer their vow to the pope's war against Frederick II.

Crusading in the Iberian peninsula was probably less contentious. Here the enemy were, as in the East, Muslims, and the reconquest of the peninsula from the forces of Islam could be presented as the liberation of Christians living under Islamic rule. From the start of the Reconquista in the eleventh century, French knights had always seen the campaigns led by the Christian kings of Castile and Aragon with papal support as spiritually meritorious; indeed, one reason for the popularity of the First Crusade with

Provençal-speaking knights may well have been their familiarity with the concept of holy war against Muslims. Spanish campaigns in the twelfth century, for example against Lisbon, Tortosa and Almeria, relied on a variety of northern European and Italian participants, and the campaign that resulted in the resounding victory at Las Navas de Tolosa in 1212 was preached all over western Europe as a crusade. Crusading continued to be a heavy commitment by Castile and Aragon throughout the thirteenth century, as Aragon, linked since the mid-twelfth century to Catalonia, expanded its conquests into the western Mediterranean islands and the eastern Iberian coastline, while Castile pushed the Muslim 'taifa' states further and further south. By the end of the fourteenth century, only Granada was left of these autonomous states, but the ease with which its rulers could appeal for help from the North African mainland made it difficult to conquer, and it was not until 1492 that the last Muslim ruler of Granada was defeated and the 'Catholic monarchs' of Castile and Aragon, Isabella and Ferdinand, were able to enter the city as victors.

Even more far-flung European adventures borrowed from crusading terminology. A series of expeditions against the pagan peoples of Karelia and northern Finland was mooted in the fifteenth century by the 'Union of Kalmar', a confederation of the three Scandinavian kingdoms. In 1401, the pope ordered a crusade to be preached in Scandinavia against the pagan enemies of Margarethe I of Denmark (1387–1412). One rationale for such a crusade was the argument that the presence of a potentially hostile pagan people on their doorstep prevented the Scandinavian knighthood from participating in the crusade against the Turks. In fact, as long as people believed that Christendom was threatened by the presence of non-Christian peoples on its frontiers, there was no less reason for crusading against the Karelians – or even the pygmies who were thought to inhabit the lands around the polar circle and Greenland – than against the Turks. And as Christendom itself expanded its range, crusading could be justified against an increasing number of newly discovered peoples. Thus the Portuguese expeditions to the Atlantic coast of Africa in the fifteenth century were also seen as crusades, and Columbus' voyages across the Atlantic, which were of course intended to secure a viable route to the East Indies, were understood in the same general context. Given that the Portuguese expeditions were intended to locate and make contact with the kingdom of the legendary Christian emperor Prester John in Africa, and thus to revive the idea of a Christian confederation against the Islamic world, they could be fitted neatly into a traditional scheme of crusading.

Crusading continued, therefore, to be a normative feature of knightly life in medieval Europe long after the expulsion of Western Christians from the Holy Land. What had changed, of course, was the link between holy war and pilgrimage that had characterized crusading since its earliest days. Crusading had, in a sense, outgrown the need for pilgrimage as a justifying rationale. This did not mean, however, that Europeans forgot or disregarded pilgrimage to the Holy Land. Pilgrimage continued to flourish as a spiritual practice even after the loss of Acre. A number of surviving accounts by fourteenth-century pilgrims show how awkward it had become: pilgrims had to obtain a passport from the Mamluk authorities in Egypt before they could enter Jerusalem; there were tolls and entrance fees to be paid, and pilgrims complained about the poor accommodation and food made available to them. But from the 1330s, the Franciscans were granted the right by the Mamluks to establish a permanent presence on Mount Zion and in the Holy Sepulchre alongside the Orthodox clergy, and through this both controlled and facilitated pilgrimage for Latin Christians. Reading fourteenth- and fifteenth-century pilgrimage accounts can leave an ambivalent impression. Although many pilgrims express regret at the loss of Christian ownership of the holy places, few seem to regard the return of Latin Christians, or a new crusade for the recovery of the Holy Land, as a live issue.

Jerusalem and the Holy Land continued to be at the centre of Christian piety, with a strong presence both liturgically and in personal devotions. They remained an ideal for the knightly classes. Henry V's deathbed vow to lead a crusade to Jerusalem was an expression of chivalric piety rather than a serious proposal, but it was meaningful nevertheless. Crusading as an activity, however, no longer depended on the Holy Land.

9

Life on the frontier: crusader society

The crusaders who settled in the East, and their descendants over the next two hundred years, experienced lives very different from their counterparts in the West. Except for those who had grown up in southern Italy, the climate and landscape of the eastern Mediterranean must have seemed severe: extremes of heat and humidity, large arid stretches of rocky land with thin soil, desert and thick forest all within close proximity. Compared with the rich agricultural land and pasture that would have been familiar to most Westerners, this was not only an alien landscape, but one that posed basic problems of how their lives were to be organized.

Most people in the West lived in and off the countryside. The manorial economy of the West was based on the production of surpluses of a variety of crops from the labour of peasants tied to the land. Advances in agricultural technology had made the cultivation of more land with a greater variety of crops more efficient in the eleventh century throughout France, Germany and England. In the Mediterranean, however, the thinner soil and lighter rainfall resulted in less productive farming, and the explosion in population seen in western and northern Europe was therefore less apparent here. For most of the new settlers in the East, the very different nature of the land itself meant that new methods of social organization were needed. The land could not support large aristocratic households on food surpluses in the same way as in the West. Contemporary travellers in the East report quite a wide variety of crops being grown – olives, dates, figs, beans, carobs, apples, grapes – but wheat, the staple of the Western medieval diet, had to be imported in large quantities from Cyprus and Sicily. Furthermore, the relative lack of pasture meant that it was difficult to support the herds that provided meat to the aristocracy of the West. Sheep and goats could survive, but there was little game of the variety or high meat content that kept such populations going throughout the long European winters, and religious dietary laws meant that pigs, a common sight in every Western village, were much less common in a land in which the majority of the population was not Christian.

Eastern Mediterranean society was fuelled less by local food production than by trade. The coastal cities of antiquity – Beirut, Tyre, Sidon, Tripoli – had continued to thrive in the Arab-dominated early Middle Ages, and under the crusaders Jaffa and Acre joined them in commercial importance. These cities provided markets for the flourishing trade across the Mediterranean with the Italian mercantile centres of Pisa, Genoa and Venice, and increasingly in the thirteenth century Marseilles and Barcelona. Western demand for Eastern luxury goods such as silk, glass and spices, for which these ports were conduits to the trade of the Indian Ocean and Red Sea, kept the ports prosperous, and it was on this economic base, rather than agriculture, that the Crusader States began to enjoy a high standard of living. The political context of the early settlement also contributed toward the development of urban life. Much of the focus of military activity in the reign of Baldwin I (1100–18) was the conquest of the coastal cities, because these were wealth providers. The relative difficulty of supporting large military households from the land meant that Godfrey (1099–1100) and Baldwin tended to grant their followers not only landed estates but also fiefs composed of commercial privileges or urban property. The capture of a city like Acre provided opportunities to endow more knights more quickly with incomes that could help them support military households than could be gained from the relatively slow process of dominating the countryside. Consequently, crusader society tended to become more urban than rural, and the ready availability of consumable luxuries in the cities meant that the standards of living in the cities were higher than in the countryside. In the West, even great lords lived in accommodation that must have been uncomfortable and cold, designed as it was for security rather than ease of living. Visitors to the East were astonished at the comforts of houses built around central courtyards, with fountains, soft furnishings in the rooms, glass in the windows and even, in a city like Antioch, running water. We know something of what cities in the Crusader States would have looked like and what it must have been like to live in them from both archaeological and textual evidence. In the honey-coloured stone houses and narrow cobbled streets in the old cities of Acre and Jerusalem we can still see the medieval towns of the eastern Mediterranean. The main streets of the old city of Jerusalem, scarcely changed since the Byzantine city of the sixth century, still preserve the shop fronts of the medieval suq; in some places, inscriptions etched into the stone still indicate the ownership of the shop in the twelfth century.

The major cities of the Crusader States – Antioch, Tripoli, Tyre, Acre, Sidon, Beirut – were thriving commercial and cultural centres. They could only have become, and remained so, with outside help. From the start of crusading, Italian cities had played an important role in securing the coastal cities that formed the economic heart of the Crusader States. Genoa, Venice, Pisa and Amalfi, the four major players in eastern Mediterranean trade with the West, had municipal forms of government that privileged trade. They saw the potential of the Crusader States as early as 1099 and individually continued to supply naval support for the campaigns of Baldwin I and Baldwin II to capture the coastline. The reason for this support was what they demanded in return.

The most spectacular result can be seen in the so-called 'Pact of Warmund' of 1123, an agreement made between Venice and Warmund, patriarch of Jerusalem and at that time regent of the kingdom of Jerusalem while Baldwin II was in captivity. The pact, made to reward the Venetians for their help in capturing Tyre, gave them a whole quarter of the city to govern themselves. Here the Venetians had their warehouses, markets and shops, as well as churches, houses and even law courts where Venetian law was observed. By the time the first kingdom of Jerusalem came to an end, most of the port cities had Venetian, Genoese and Pisan quarters, and during the thirteenth century the presence of merchants from the new western Mediterranean commercial centres of Marseilles and Barcelona became increasingly marked. These mercantile quarters were not restricted to the Crusader States: there were similar quarters in Constantinople and Alexandria. Their purpose was not only to house foreign merchants and their families, but to give their home cities control of the trade passing through the quarter. It is a mark of the volume of total trade and its value to the kingdom of Jerusalem that kings were prepared to accept the loss of revenue as a result of granting these quarters.

The Western settlers did not only live in the coastal cities. They also developed new villages and expanded the agriculture and viticulture of the areas around Jerusalem and the coastal plain. Industries, such as sugar refineries, were created. Castles, especially those of the Military Orders, became administrative centres of crusader agribusiness, controlling scores of villages, vineyards and farms. Baldwin I and Fulk (1131–43) encouraged settlement from the West with the promise of free leaseholds. One of the factors that must have made settlement from the West attractive to many was the rise in social standards as well as standards of living. In the East, every Frank, or Westerner, no matter how low his or her social status, was superior socially and in the eyes of the law to the native people. In principle, the laws of the kingdom of

Jerusalem and the principality of Antioch did not recognize religious differences between those who lived under their rule. The differences were rather racial or ethnic: one was either a Frank or a non-Frank. Franks were subject to a law code designed to govern relations among themselves, and when they came into contact with non-Franks in matters where the law was involved, the law was stacked in their favour. An indication of status is given by the relative monetary value assigned to Franks and non-Franks in the sliding scale of fines for causing injury or death. The penalties for harming or killing non-Franks were lower than for Franks. The law, however, is not a particularly good guide for telling us what crusader society was actually like when it came to the treatment of non-Franks. In fact, we know remarkably little about the laws that operated in the kingdom before the thirteenth century, because the written codes and any records kept about legal cases were all lost in 1187 and had to be reconstructed in entirely new conditions from the 1190s onward. Besides this, laws often indicate idealized expectations rather than realities.

The Crusader States have, with some justice, been called a 'colonial society'. In fact, they can be said to represent Europeans' first colonial venture. Although the Crusader States do appear to have conformed to many of the forms of colonialism with which we have become familiar from subsequent histories, the use of the term is not without difficulties when applied to the medieval Western settlement of the Near East. One such difficulty concerns our expectations and attitudes based on the norms of twenty-first century Western society. Another, perhaps harder to resolve, is the assumption that it was invariably easy to tell the difference between Franks and 'natives'. For one thing, 'Franks' were themselves a mixed community. The south Norman contingent led by Bohemond on the First Crusade, for example, had been settled in southern Italy for two generations by 1095, and intermarriage with the local Italian population meant that any distinctly 'Norman' identity ascribed to them is probably as much a literary construct as a reality. Furthermore, the Western settlers in all of the Crusader States intermarried with the local Arabic-speaking and Armenian Christian population. Indeed, they had no alternative but to marry local women, because the numbers of Frankish women who accompanied the crusade and survived were too small to maintain the Frankish population. After a generation, therefore, the term 'Frank' was already beginning to have largely a legal and social meaning rather than a racial one. The example of intermarriage was set right at the top of society. Baldwin I and Baldwin II both married Armenian women, as did many other Frankish lords who had originally settled in north Syria, where there were large Armenian communities; Baldwin II's son Baldwin III, himself half-Armenian, married a Byzantine princess, as did his brother Amalric I. Although very little is known about marriage practices lower down the social scale, the presence of Greek and even Arab names as urban property owners in Acre, Tyre and other cities indicates an integrated community by the thirteenth century.

Whatever the degree of racial integration may have been, there is no doubt that Franks developed a hybrid culture that borrowed from what they found in the East. At the most basic level this took the form of adopting Eastern diet, hygiene and clothing, all of which were remarked on by Western visitors and Arabs alike. Usamah ibn Munqidh, an Arab aristocrat whose lordship over Shaizar, in north-west Syria, made him a neighbour of both the Aleppans and the Franks, recorded in a series of vignettes the degrees of adaptation of Franks who had themselves been born in the East. Remarking ruefully on the rough treatment he had himself received at the hands of a group of newly arrived Templars, he observed that the longer they had lived in the East, the closer to genuinely civilized standards of conduct the Franks became. The same observation was made, with less approval, by crusaders coming out to the East for the first time. On the Third Crusade, Angevin and French crusaders mocked the native-born

Franks in the East as *pullani* or *poulains,* a term of obscure meaning but intended as an insult concerning their moral character and integrity. James of Vitry, who arrived to take up his post as bishop of Acre in 1216, was scandalized by the loose morals he found in the city among the Westerners, which he attributed to their having lived for so long alongside the native people. Looking back in the 1320s at the reasons for the fall of the Crusader States, the Dominican friar William Adam pointed the finger at the very worst among all the inhabitants of the East – those born of mixed Frankish and native-Christian parentage. This kind of prejudice against mixed-race Franks is comparable with the attitude towards Anglo-Indians of mixed descent in the Raj.

Among Franks in the East, however, Eastern culture seems to have been highly prized. It must have helped that the most powerful patrons, the royal family, were well disposed to the arts of the Byzantine world. When King Fulk wanted to commission a deluxe book of Psalms for his wife, Queen Melisende, which may have been a gesture of political reconciliation rather than of marital affection, he chose artists who were either Byzantines or Byzantine-trained. The *Melisende Psalter*, one of the most exquisite of twelfth-century manuscripts, is an early example of a hybrid artistic style that would become characteristic of the Crusader States in the thirteenth century, in which Byzantine techniques, styles and iconography were borrowed for Western usages. Sometimes such manuscripts were even bilingual, with Latin or French appearing alongside Greek or Armenian: further evidence of the multiple usages of these books. Likewise, when the clergy who ran the shrine churches wanted to decorate them, they chose Eastern techniques, materials and styles. Mosaic, a technique unknown in the West outside Sicily, which imported Byzantine artists, was used to decorate the interiors of the Church of the Holy Sepulchre and the Church of the Nativity in Bethlehem. Not all of this cultural traffic was in one direction. In Cyprus, where the Frankish presence under the Lusignan monarchs lasted until the late-fifteenth century and under the Venetians for a further hundred years, many wall paintings in rural churches show distinctly Western influences in style and iconography, even where the subject matter is Orthodox. The most striking example of this hybrid culture that developed in the Crusader States is a series of icons, many of which survive in the monastery of St Katherine on Mount Sinai. Since icons are quintessentially part of Greek Orthodox religious practice rather than Western, when we are confronted with icons depicting Western saints unknown in the Orthodox calendar, or with Latin inscriptions, we can be sure that these were made for Frankish patrons. Enough of these survive to be confident that there were workshops turning them out for such patrons, probably in Acre. Clearly, then, Westerners with money to spend chose Byzantine art forms, just as religious communities valued the high pres-tige that Byzantine art signalled. Was this anything more than an aesthetic choice, or were patrons commissioning such icons because they had also been influenced by the usages to which they were put by Greek Orthodox Christians? In cases where the patrons might have been the offspring of mixed Frankish and native parentage, this is certainly plausible. Westerners discovered and venerated a new set of saints and shrines and simply added them to existing devotions.

Both this socio-cultural hybridity and the reactions against it took time to develop. At the time of the first settlement of Franks in the East, the settlers probably did not perceive distinctions between themselves and the native peoples to be so remarkable. Some of them were used to living among other peoples with dif-ferent customs, laws and religious practices. Equally important, for most Europeans, there was as yet no definite sense of belonging to a particular nationality or racial group. Although people were conscious of language groups to which they belonged, nation states in anything like a modern sense did not yet exist – either in the West or in the eastern Mediterranean. This made the prospect of settlement in new territories less like emigration and more like, for example, the westward expansion across America in the nineteenth century. Newcomers found a place in a layered and complex landscape, and relations between Frankish newcomers and the native inhabitants were governed by a matrix in which marriage, political patronage, religious affiliation and professional identity all played a part.

The native population of the Crusader States was mixed ethnically and in terms of religious and cultural identities. The Seljuqs were a fairly small military caste ruling over the indigenous inhabitants of the lands they themselves had conquered in the mid-eleventh century, who constituted Arabs, both Muslim and Christian, Greeks and Armenians. The Arabic-speaking Christians were the descendants of the inhabitants of the Roman, subse-quently Byzantine-ruled provinces of Palestine and Syria. Many, but not all, had converted to Islam either in the seventh century or in later waves of Islamicization, but even those who remained Christian spoke Arabic as their native language. Most of the Christians lived in the region of Jerusalem and Bethlehem, or in Galilee. In the Holy Land, the majority of the population were probably Arab Muslims, but in the principality of Antioch and the county of Edessa, the majority of the natives were Syrian Christians or Armenians, who had settled in large numbers in south-east Asia Minor and the Euphrates–Tigris basin in the eleventh century.

The conquest of the Holy Land by the crusaders was not accomplished in a single stroke in 1099, because the main cen-tres of population, the coastal cities, were taken one by one in a series of campaigns by the early kings. By 1112, when Sidon fell to Baldwin I, most of them were in Christian hands, but Tyre held out until 1124 and Ascalon until 1153. This meant that there were still large Muslim populations in the cities for the first few years of the kingdom of Jerusalem's existence. The fate of these populations depended on the manner in which the cities came into Christian hands. If they surrendered, they were likely to be spared the worst excesses that had befallen Jerusalem itself in July 1099, but where Muslim garrisons held out for long sieges, little mercy was shown to the Muslim populations. Those left alive after the cities had been sacked were usually enslaved or exiled. Wealthy families might be able to buy their passage to Damascus, Aleppo or Egypt, but most were probably forcibly resettled in the interior of the kingdom on terms of extreme servility. This was partly because the Franks wanted to live in and profit from the commercial potential of the cities themselves, but also because they needed rural manpower to work on the land. The consequences of this policy for Muslims who came under crusader control could hardly have been more profound. Urban elites and artisans became peasants, and the legal and religious schools in Jerusalem and other cities vanished. Mosques in all the cities were converted into churches. The loss of an Islamic intelligentsia meant that western Syria and Palestine became even more provincial outposts of Islam.

The situation was very different from that in the other parts of the Islamic world that became subject to Christian domin-ation. In Sicily, where Muslims remained the majority of the population in the west of the island under the Norman kings, the financial administration remained Arabic, and both Muslim Sicilians and North Africans were fundamental to the Norman royal bureaucracy. In Spain, Muslim cities and regions that came under the control of the Christian kingdoms of the north retained much of their former character through the grants by kings of new inclusive law codes, and there was no wholesale attempt to sideline, do away with or forcibly exile Muslim populations. In the Crusader States alone could Muslims find no role in the new regimes other than as slaves, servants or agricultural labour-ers. Even where they were valued for skills of artisanship such as metalwork, they seem to have been retained by Franks on these conditions. There are two main reasons for this different approach in the East. First, unlike in Sicily and Spain, there was in the Levant no pre-existing state bureaucracy in the conquered territories that the local Arab population might have been useful in maintaining; the Franks simply set up their own on Western models. Second, where Arab expertise was needed in administration, or for translating and interpreting, or for medical provision, the Arabic-speaking Christian population rather than Muslims were used.

As far as we can tell, the settlement patterns in the interior of the kingdom kept Muslims and Christians – even Arabic-speaking Christians – apart. Resettled Muslims occupied their own villages, largely living in self-regulated communities under their own chiefs and using Islamic law and customs. As long as they performed the work required by their Frankish landlords, and did not try to leave the land, they were probably left alone. There are examples of attempted rebellion, but these are few and far between in the context of the huge disruption caused by the resettlement. They were permitted freedom of worship, and no attempt was made to convert them to Christianity. We know of some individual cases of conversion, doubtless where Muslims thought they could advance themselves by such a move, but there was no such policy. Indeed, in the thirteenth century, Frankish lords were taken to task by the papacy for failing to stimulate conversion of Muslims. One reason for this failure was that Muslims who converted could no longer be held as slaves. For most rural Muslims, their conditions of life probably resembled those of the peasantry throughout the Mediterranean. Ibn Jubayr famously remarked on the relative comfort in which the Muslim villagers he saw in the Galilee lived under crusader rule – far more easily, he thought, than their neighbours in Damascene territory. Muslim villagers were taxed, both on their produce and by a head-tax, but unlike Latin Christians they were not subject to tithes payable to the Church. Nevertheless, the ease with which Saladin swept through the kingdom and restored Islamic worship in the cities suggests that he was welcomed by large swathes of the native population, and a Syrian Christian account of the conquest of Edessa by Zengi in 1144 leaves no doubt as to the unpopularity of Frankish rule there, even among Syrian Christians.

The native Christian population suffered mixed fortunes under crusader rule. On the one hand, the fear of persecution under which they had lived before the First Crusade was at an end. On the other, the crusaders brought with them their own Latin Christianity, and the shrines and holy places came into the hands of the Latin Church rather than the Greek or Syrian Orthodox. With the shrines came also income streams in the form of pilgrims' offerings and bequests from pious laity. Pilgrimage from the West had been increasing steadily since the 1030s, but once the obstructions put in the way of pilgrims by the Seljuqs had been removed in 1099, it flowed to a torrent, and throughout the twelfth century pilgrims in large numbers visited Jerusalem, Bethlehem, Nazareth and the small Galilee villages associated with Christ's ministry. The economy of the Latin Church in the Holy Land was founded on pilgrim traffic, but since it was the Latins who controlled the shrine churches, even in shrines such as the Holy Sepulchre where the Greek Orthodox and other native Christian communities also had a presence, most of the money spent by pilgrims went into Latin coffers. The Latin Church also controlled the institutions and hierarchy of the Church. Although most of the Christians in the Crusader States were Greek Orthodox, with a very few exceptions, for short periods, all the bishops were Latin clergy. Greek Orthodox parishes continued to function in towns and villages, and sometimes they even shared churches with the Latins, but the obedience of Orthodox clergy to their Latin bishop was required. In principle at least, this meant that Orthodox customs and practices were brought into line with Latin, but in practice it is doubtful whether this happened. James of Vitry complained in the early thirteenth century that native clergy in Acre and Sidon were continuing to administer the Eucharist and other sacraments according to their own traditions rather than following Latin customs.

The so-called 'Separated Churches' of the Armenians and Syrian Orthodox, which were not in communion with either the Latin or Greek Orthodox Churches, were largely left alone by the Western settlers. Because the Latin and Separated Churches did not recognize each others' sacraments, they continued to appoint their own bishops for their communities. Both Greek Orthodox and Separated Churches also maintained their own monasteries under crusader rule. The Syrian Orthodox monasteries were mostly in northern Syria, but by the middle of the thirteenth century they were finding it difficult to make ends meet. In contrast, many Greek Orthodox monasteries thrived in the Crusader States. Some of these, like the monastery of St Sabas in the Kidron Valley, in the spectacular but arid landscape of the Judaean Desert, had been celebrated as centres of learning and spirituality for centuries, and attracted Western as well as Orthodox pilgrims. In the early thirteenth century, the remote monastery on Mount Sinai, founded in the sixth century, adopted the dedication of St Katherine and began to display her relics, which were thought to have healing properties. The monastery grew in size and prestige, and in the fourteenth century became a regular stop on the itinerary of Western pilgrims. St Katherine, according to tradition an Alexandrian Christian of the third century whose cult had been quite obscure until the twelfth century, swiftly became one of the best-loved of all saints in the Middle Ages.

Cultural and artistic life in the Crusader States was centred on the decorative programmes in the shrine churches. From the 1120s onward, the settlers began to rebuild and enlarge the most important shrine, the Church of the Holy Sepulchre in Jerusalem. This entailed not only new building but the commissioning of new mosaic and fresco cycles for the various chapels within the church. Likewise, the Church of the Nativity in Bethlehem,

THE HOLY SEPULCHRE

The tomb of Jesus does not seem to have been venerated by the earliest Christians, and it was not until the fourth century and the extensive building programme launched in Jerusalem by Emperor Constantine (306–37) that a church was built on the site. Constantine's church was in fact a complex commemorating both Calvary, the place of the crucifixion, and, close by, the cave tomb where Jesus' body had been laid after his death. The tomb became the site of particular veneration because it was the physical symbol of the central belief of Christianity: the resurrection. The Anastasis (Resurrection) Church, known in the West as the Church of the Holy Sepulchre, was destroyed by the Caliph al-Hakim in 1009, but rebuilt on a smaller scale in the course of the eleventh century and then enlarged by the crusaders in the twelfth. The church as it survives today is largely the church that the crusaders rebuilt. Its main feature is the small chapel in the middle of the rotunda in which the grave slab is still preserved from the first-century cave tomb. This chapel is still the focal point of Christian devotions in the church. Calvary forms a separate chapel within the church, as does the crypt chapel dedicated to the discovery of the true cross by Helena, Constantine's mother. Under crusader rule, a chapter of Western canons staffed the church as its cathedral clergy, but Greek Orthodox, Armenian and Egyptian Copts also maintained their own altars in the church.

the Church of the Annunciation in Nazareth and various other notable churches, such as Mount Zion in Jerusalem and Abu Ghosh (Emmaus), benefited from grand decorative programmes. The work on the Holy Sepulchre alone, which was finished in 1149, took over twenty years. During most of the twelfth century, therefore, artists, sculptors, mosaicists and artisans associated with church building must have been working in large numbers in the

Crusader States. As we have already seen, the visual culture of the Crusader States was dominated by Eastern Christian influence on Western forms and styles.

Intellectual life lagged behind the West in some respects. The late-eleventh and twelfth centuries were exciting times for the growth of intellectual life in France, England, Germany, Italy and Spain. Schools of higher learning, associated with cathedrals and nominally run as part of diocesan activities, pushed back the frontiers of understanding in philosophy, theology and natural sciences with extraordinary speed. By 1200, many of these had developed into universities – self-governing scholarly communities with set courses of study based on the corpus of Aristotelian texts that was being newly discovered in the West. Aristotle's voluminous works covering all aspects of scientific and social knowledge had been preserved in Greek and Arabic, but in 1100 only a few existed in Latin, the language of intellectual discourse in the West. Because of this, scholars who could translate texts and commentaries from Greek or Arabic were highly prized. Although most of this activity took place in Islamic Spain, where a degree of mutual co-operation between scholars was a strong feature of intellectual life, some of it took place in the Crusader States. The Italian Burgundio of Pisa was active as a translator of Greek patristic texts and of Aristotle in twelfth-century Antioch. Some of this learning rubbed off on Latin higher clergy. Amalric, patriarch of Antioch from 1142 to 1180, requested translations of Greek works from Burgundio and his compatriot Hugo Eteriano, who was based in Constantinople. But there were no centres of higher learning in the Crusader States comparable with those in the West, and although there must have been schools based in the main cathedral centres, young men who wanted an advanced intellectual life, such as William of Tyre and the future patriarch of Jerusalem, Heraclius, had to go to Paris to acquire it.

If we take a less Western-centred view of intellectual life, the Crusader States look rather more impressive. Although Islamic centres of legal and religious scholarship were lost in 1099, Arabic Christian intellectuals continued to work in Antioch and other cities and in Orthodox monasteries. Antioch was an intellectual centre in the eleventh century, with a reputation for medical knowledge. Ibn Butlan, a Baghdadi Christian who settled there in the 1040s, founded a hospital and wrote medical treatises that combined Greek and Arabic medical theory. Symeon Seth, a Greek-speaking Antiochene, dedicated a medical treatise to the Byzantine emperor in the 1070s, and the tradition seems to have been maintained into the thirteenth century, when the Syrian Christian Theodore of Antioch wrote his own treatise on health for the Emperor Frederick II. Some of the Orthodox and Eastern Christian higher clergy were considerable intellectuals. Athanasios, Greek patriarch of Antioch (1157–71), wrote biblical commentaries and hagiographical treatises. Michael, his younger Syrian Orthodox contemporary (1166–99), also wrote biblical commentaries as well as the great chronicle for which he is best known. There were also notable Jewish scholars in the Crusader States, such as Moses ben Nahman, an émigré rabbi from Spain who settled in the East and wrote a distinguished commentary on the Torah.

Cities such as Acre, Antioch and Tyre were among the most cosmopolitan anywhere in the Mediterranean world. For the two hundred years or so that the mainland Crusader States remained in existence, they brought together mixed populations of Westerners, speaking French, Italian, German, Catalan and Provençal, with Arabs, Greeks, Armenians, Georgians, Jews from Spain and North Africa, merchants from Damascus and Baghdad, and pilgrims from as far away as India, Ethiopia, Russia and Iceland. Under Western rule, the cities of the Levantine coast carried on the mixed international commercial life that they had known since the time of the Seleucids. It was the final flourish of an ancient civilization, but it did not outlast the crusaders. When the Mamluks completed their conquest of the Crusader

States in 1291, they destroyed the coastal cities so they could no longer provide a foothold for any new crusading expedition. The German pilgrim Ludolph of Sudheim, who came to the Holy Land as a pilgrim in the fourteenth century, describes how he wandered through the ruins of what had been marble halls and palaces a hundred years earlier.

10

The transformation
of the Crusades

One reason why crusading proved so elastic a concept, and thus why it was so easy to extend it to activities far beyond what Urban II had envisaged in 1095, was that there was no precise word to describe it. It is true that we find the term 'signed with the cross' to describe participants on Urban II's expedition as early as Albert of Aachen, who was writing in the 1120s, but it does not seem to have caught on until the very end of the twelfth century. Moreover, it did not develop into a noun to describe the events in which such knights were engaged. Urban II had not given the expedition he launched in 1095 any particular title, but he had said that in spiritual terms the expedition was the equivalent of a pilgrimage to Jerusalem, and it was logical therefore for contemporary authors to refer to it as a pilgrimage and to the participants as pilgrims. This was probably the commonest word to describe what we call crusading throughout the medieval period. Other terms used varied from the circumlocution 'the business of the cross' to the neutral 'expedition'.

Our word 'crusade' in its current form first appears only in the sixteenth century, in a Spanish text – which means that it developed in the vernacular, rather than in the language of ecclesiastical authority, Latin. The first appearance of the word 'crusade' is a significant moment in the history of crusading. It marks the point at which people writing about holy war felt the need for a single word to encompass the phenomenon. By implication, before

that moment, the activity was defined simply by its reception: in other words, what mattered was not what the activity was called but the fact that it had been authorized by papal preaching and that it carried with it certain spiritual benefits. The coining of the single term indicates that writers were reflecting on what the phenomenon of holy war meant in a wider context.

This context was provided by the Reformation. For those who questioned the legitimacy of papal authority and the papal office itself, the concept of the crusade as defined by papal authorization made no sense. This did not necessarily mean, however, that the idea of holy war fell into disrepute among all the reformers. There had always been a strong element of lay piety and even initiative in crusading, going back as far as the twelfth century when armed pilgrimages to Jerusalem were led by knights who were not responding to any specific papal appeal. Reformers who refused to recognize the papacy's role in legitimizing holy war did not by the same token wish to deny the validity of the vows that Christian knights had taken in good faith to rescue the Holy Land. Indeed, the fact that, at the time of the Protestant Reformation, the Turks were more powerful than ever caused some difficulties for reformers. Under Suleiman the Magnificent (1520–66) the Turks took the Hospitaller island of Rhodes (1522), crushed the kingdom of Hungary at Mohács (1526) and threatened Vienna. In 1570, Cyprus, ruled by the Venetians, fell to the Turks. The naval battle of Lepanto (1571), in which the Turkish advance across the Mediterranean was halted, was the first significant victory won by the combined Christian powers over the Turks in living memory, and it was celebrated in Protestant as well as Catholic Europe. The Protestant martyrologist John Foxe, writing for an English audience in the late-sixteenth century, fulminated against the pretensions of the papacy, but equally against the Turks as the forces of Islam that threatened Christian Europe. Not surprisingly, this led to a rather ambivalent attitude on his part to the Crusades.

What reformers like Foxe objected to was neither the idea of holy war, nor the defence of Christendom, but the spiritual benefits that had become inseparable from crusading since the twelfth century. Specifically, they rejected the validity of indulgences. In 1095, Urban II had simply said that the expedition to Jerusalem was the equivalent of a penitential pilgrimage to the Holy Land; in other words, that it was a temporal satisfaction for sins committed and confessed to a priest. Gradually this position widened and blurred. Pope Eugenius III's bull of 1145/6 already implied the forgiveness of sins, and as the theology of purgatory developed in the twelfth century, so did the canonical precision of the penitential system. By the sixteenth century, not only could indulgences be granted for a variety of activities, they were defined according to notional periods of time remitted in purgatory. Most pernicious of all practices, in the reformers' view, was the sale of indulgences. This was abolished during the Counter-Reformation following the Council of Trent, but not until 1567. An earlier attempt by the reform-minded pope Paul III (1534–49) to abolish crusading indulgences failed, and his successors in the 1560s and 1570s, even after their sale had been abolished, continued to grant indulgences for crusading against the Turks. The theology underlying such initiatives had not changed much since Innocent III (1198–1216), but it was a theology derived from patristic scholarship rather than directly from Scripture. Reformers, both Protestant and Catholic, were more informed by the New Testament and especially by the humanistic learning that had made possible a direct approach to Scripture in its original languages, Hebrew and Greek. At the same time, the study of secular law led scholars to challenge the canon-law assumptions that had supported crusade preaching in earlier centuries. Doubts were expressed both about the legitimacy of extending Christian authority over non-Christians in natural law, and about the place of religious causation in war.

If the intellectual climate seemed to be shifting away from crusading, it remained a popular subject for writers. The period

from about 1550 to 1650 saw a burst of historical writing, in the form of chronicles, national and regional histories, and popular literature for performance such as plays and ballads. Much of this dealt with the Crusades, and not always in a negative fashion. Printing meant that historical sources could be made available to larger numbers of scholars than ever before. The scholarly collation and editing of earlier chronicles enabled writers to read and compare different sources in ways that had not been possible when only manuscript copies were available, and then only in monastic libraries. It was in the sixteenth and early seventeenth centuries that the study of the Crusades as an historical phenomenon became a reality.

In England, Richard Knolles' *Historie of the Turkes* (1603) longed for the re-creation of a united Europe with common religious goals that could push back the frontiers of Islam. By the 1620s and '30s, the English encounter with the Ottomans became more direct than ever before, as the founding of the Levant Company took English merchants to Istanbul and Aleppo. The immediate threat to Europe might have been over, but the activities of the Barbary Coast corsairs, who came as far north as the Devon coast, reminded the English of their vulnerability. It was in this context that the first full history of the Crusades in English was written, Thomas Fuller's *Historie of the Holy Warre* (1639). Fuller, an Anglican clergyman, had no doubt about the dangers of militant Islam, but he was sceptical of the claims of any Church to deal with them. Instead, like other Protestant writers, he looked to state governments to protect their people through the application of rational defensive war policies where necessary. He was virulent in his criticism of papal use of crusade indulgences and preaching against their political enemies, and scornful of, as he saw them, stories of miracles and relics designed to excite popular emotions.

In some ways the preference for national rather than papal control of warfare cut across the religious divide in Europe. When

Pope Paul III had tried to abolish the crusade indulgence in the mid-sixteenth century, it was the opposition of the Spanish crown that prevented any such reform, because the Habsburgs saw the crusade as a necessary instrument of their imperial policy. The notion of crusading as a living embodiment of the Church's authority continued to find supporters in Catholic Europe, long after it had been rejected by Protestants. A generation after Fuller, the French Jesuit Louis Maimbourg published his *History of the Crusades* (1675). Maimbourg, who was writing only a few years before the Turkish threat was finally dispelled at the siege of Vienna (1683), was widely read in crusading sources and fully believed in the validity of the enterprise of crusading. Yet he was also a fervent royalist, for whom King Louis XIV was the natural successor of his great crusading forefathers of hundreds of years earlier. Maimbourg regarded the Crusades as an important part of Christian Europe's heritage, and where Fuller saw waste and folly, he saw glory and noble sacrifice to a higher cause than territorial politics. Telling the story of the Crusades, however, was not just a matter of informing readers of uplifting moral tales from Europe's past. History has rarely been written without service to some agenda on the part of the writer, and Maimbourg's was the glorification of the French monarchy. Although, in fact, French kings had been signally ineffective when it came to achieving anything on crusade, between the 1140s and the 1330s there was an almost unbroken line of French royal leadership of crusading.

The theme of crusading as a French royal function – almost a destiny – fell into some disrepute during the period of 'philosophical' history in the eighteenth century, when Enlightenment writers such as Voltaire and Diderot, followed in Britain by Hume and Gibbon, took a rationalist and disapproving attitude. In some ways they adopted the same attitude as Fuller, considering crusading wasteful and foolhardy; but whereas to Fuller the Turkish threat was still real, and religion not an inherently implausible reason for going to war, Enlightenment writers could not understand

how their ancestors had been so foolish or misguided. Famously, Diderot's *Encyclopedia* piece described the Crusades as a quest for 'a rock not worth a single drop of blood'. In fact, had he but known it, there were medieval thinkers – the twelfth-century author Ralph Niger being one example – who had expressed similar sentiments; but underlying the Enlightenment project was an invincible sense of superiority over the medieval past. Religious 'enthusiasm' – to use Gibbon's disparaging term – came in for particular scorn.

Yet by the 1820s, European culture had begun a new appreciation of all things medieval. The development of a Gothic sensibility and aesthetic, seen for example in romantic poetry, in the enjoyment of medieval ruins and in historical painting, allowed a new look at crusading. The early nineteenth century thus saw a mixture of approaches. Maimbourg found a successor in Joseph Michaud's *Histoire des Croisades,* originally published in 1817 but revised at various points in the nineteenth century. Like Maimbourg, a royalist, Michaud was writing for the generation that saw the restoration and rehabilitation of the monarchy in France. In emphasizing the crusading glories of the French kings of the past, Michaud was giving the new Bourbon dynasty the same associations. These can be seen not only in historical writing, but equally in the huge series of paintings dating from the 1830s in the 'Crusading Hall' in the palace at Versailles, which traced the history of the Crusades as a distinctly French and monarchical enterprise. Pride of place in this medieval fantasy is given to the French pope, Urban II, and to the crusading kings Louis VII and Louis IX. The general tenor represented by this cycle of paintings, in which the Crusades were heroic enterprises in which virtue and villainy clashed, also informed the popular literature of the day in both French and English. Sir Walter Scott's medieval novels, particularly *Ivanhoe* (1820) and *The Talisman* (1825), luxuriate in an imagined medieval past no less heroic and epic than the Versailles paintings. Just as the paintings tell us more about the search for

Figure 8   From a set of four earthenware floor-tiles from Chertsey Abbey, Surrey, made in the mid-thirteenth century, and depicting combat between Richard the Lionheart and a Muslim warrior who may be intended to represent Saladin. (Source: Wikimedia Commons)

a role for the restored French royal dynasty, so Scott's stories are really about the virtues and dreams of the Scottish gentry of his day. They proved not only hugely popular but also influential, and of course they formed part of a sentimental cultural ambience that Victorian Britain embraced willingly.

Scott has even been credited with creating the modern image of Saladin as a chivalric hero of Islam, though European writers had been praising Saladin's personal virtue since the thirteenth century, and even Gibbon saw him as an exception to the irrational folly that characterized the Crusades on both sides. In fact, Saladin's achievements had never been forgotten in the Islamic world. Only a little earlier than the period when European writers like Matthias Kretz (1532), Matthew Dresser (1536–1607), Foxe and Knolles were reconsidering the place of crusading in their history, the Arab writer Mujir al-Din al-'Ulaymi (1456–1522) was compiling a history of Jerusalem and Hebron in which Saladin plays a major role. Moreover, the spread of manuscripts of this

work indicate that it was widely read throughout the Islamic world. Among Muslim writers, the memory of the Crusades continued to be traumatic even when there was no longer any realistic possibility of a European attempt to reconquer the Holy Land. Walter Scott's romanticized view of the conflict between Christian Europe and the Islamic world was one of a number of nineteenth-century responses to the Crusades. In both the Islamic and Western worlds, the Crusades took on new resonances in the changing political conditions of the modern nation state. The French annexation of Algeria in 1830, and the subsequent creation of a new French Empire in largely Muslim-populated lands – following as it did on Napoleon's short-lived invasion of Egypt a generation earlier – was consciously compared to the Crusader States of the twelfth and thirteenth centuries. French colonialism in the nineteenth and early twentieth centuries was seen by many French historians of the time as a return to the natural destiny of the French nation to bring the benefits of civilization to Islamic peoples. Napoleon III, in establishing a French protectorate over Syria and Lebanon, explicitly told his soldiers to show that they were 'the dignified children of those heroes who gloriously brought the banner of Christ to that land' – ignoring the fact that there had been Christian communities there before the banner of Christ ever reached Gaul.

Not surprisingly, such attitudes met with resistance toward the end of the nineteenth century and the beginning of the twentieth from the nascent Arab nationalist movement. Inspired in part by European nationalist movements, Arabs in the Near East and North Africa began to support attempts to dismantle the Ottoman Empire. In this political context, figures such as Saladin had more to offer than simply being embodiments of courtesy and virtue. He became instead an authentic 'national' hero of liberation. The celebrated visit of Kaiser Wilhelm II to Damascus in 1898, when he donated funds for the rebuilding of Saladin's tomb, was one of a series of gestures towards the past,

but Arab nationalists were quick to see how it could be used to serve their cause symbolically. Nowhere was this use of Saladin more evident in the twentieth century than in the Syria of the Assad regime from 1979 onward. Portrayals of President Hafez al-Assad alongside Saladin, and the construction of the dramatic Saladin Monument next to the walls of the old city of Damascus, made explicit links between the present and the past. In 2009, the opening performance of an extraordinary dance–drama at the Syrian National Theatre in Damascus was introduced by a speech by the Minister of Culture in which the importance of Saladin to Syrians as an inspirational figure for today's struggle against Western imperialism was made patently clear. In the contested territory of Palestine, a similar message was delivered in 1992 by the President of Birzeit University, Gabi Baramki, in opening a conference entitled 'The Frankish Wars and their Influences'. The 'Frankish Wars' were of course the Crusades, and an explicit link was made between the territorial coverage of the State of Israel and Crusader rule over the same territory eight hundred years previously. Conversely, Israeli scholars in the period after the creation of the state of Israel in 1948 made comparisons between crusader rule and the British Mandate from which they had just liberated themselves. In general, the attitude of Western scholars to the Crusades was similarly negative in the generation after 1945. The retreat from imperialism in Britain and France seemed to provide a contemporary backdrop against which historical events could be judged. The rebuilding of Europe, and movements of self-determination in colonial Africa and Asia, offered visions of a future in which reminders of the West's aggression against non-Christians centuries before were an embarrassment.

In the first half of the twentieth century, however, it was not only Middle Eastern politics that mobilized the Crusades in service of contemporary agendas. The struggle for nationhood and freedom from Ottoman rule won by Serbs and Montenegrins in the Balkan Wars of 1912–13 was seen as revenge for the Ottoman

victory over the Serbs at Kosovo in 1389. The first great battle of World War I, the German victory over the Russians at Tannenberg in August 1914, was seen by some in Germany as revenge for the defeat of the Teutonic Knights at the hands of Alexander Nevsky in the 'Battle of the Ice' in 1242; Eisenstein's great film *Alexander Nevsky* (1938) likewise played on Soviet fears of Nazi expansion eastward by retelling the story of the battle. The Spanish dictator Francisco Franco, using his alliance with the Catholic hierarchy, represented himself as a 'crusading' liberator of Spain from anti-clerical Republicanism in the same way as the Christian kings had 'liberated' the Iberian peninsula from Muslim rule in the Middle Ages. That he and his propagandists misrepresented the historical character of the Reconquista was beside the point. The past has always been fair game in political propaganda.

Perhaps because of distaste for such contemporary associations, the Crusades as a topic of historical study became somewhat marginal within medieval history more generally for a generation from the 1950s onward. Readers who wanted to gain an overview of the Crusades had relatively little in the way of introductory or general books from which to choose: Sir Steven Runciman's classic *History of the Crusades* (1951), Hans Eberhard Mayer's *The Crusades,* originally published in German but translated into English in 1972, supplemented by the solid but indigestible multi-volume 'Philadelphia' *History of the Crusades* (1958–89), provided the standard fare. In contrast, the first decade of the twenty-first century saw an unparalleled explosion of general books about the Crusades, reflecting new growth in scholarly and public interest across Europe, the Middle East and North America.

Crusading studies are now more diverse and extensive than ever before. They are also just as important as ever. The rise of extremist political and religious ideologies in the 1990s produced new rhetorical frameworks for violence in West and South Asia, parts of post-communist Europe and America, in which the Crusades have once more made an appearance. Statements made by the

al-Qaeda leadership from the late 1990s onward, and by the US president himself in 2001 and 2002 in response to the al-Qaeda terrorist attacks on the USA in September 2001, both deployed 'crusade', though intending opposing meanings. That both did so in ignorance of crusading history did not matter for the political effect of their rhetoric. Indeed, ignorance – or at best only superficial knowledge – of history has led some commentators to take the Crusades as a normative matrix for relations between 'East' and 'West'.

The assumption that relations between 'the Islamic world' and 'the West' inevitably embody a 'clash of civilizations' is problematic for several reasons. The most obvious is that it cannot be supported by the historical evidence. Before the late-eleventh century, Christian Europe, which comprised groups of coexisting communities observing different cultures, laws and religions, was untroubled by the parallel existence of Islam and Muslims. If Christians in the West thought about Islam at all, they regarded it as a heretical offshoot of Christianity. Only when a group of ideals about pilgrimage, penance and how a militarized aristocracy might use arms justly were melded together and applied to concerns over the security of Christians in the East did what we call 'crusading' begin. Even then, the problem to which Urban II's expedition was seen as a solution was not about Islam as a religion or Islamic culture, but about the Seljuq Turks and their perceived conduct. Before the middle of the thirteenth century, hardly anyone in the West wrote or thought about the existence of Islam or the Islamic world as a problem in itself. Theology and religious sensibilities therefore followed in the wake of a specific historical situation in the 1090s. Moreover, to think of 'the West' as the same thing as 'the Christian world', and 'the East' as corresponding to 'the Islamic world' also flouts the historical evidence. Large communities of Christians and Jews lived under Islamic rule for centuries before any military action in the name of Christendom was seen to be necessary. During certain periods,

they suffered persecution or were subject to harsh penal codes, both before the 1090s and after crusading effectively ended. One of these periods occurred at a time when the leadership of the Christian West thought that military action provided a suitable response. But even during the period when crusading was a normative feature of European society, Christians dealt with Muslims in other ways than fighting – they traded with them, corresponded with them, shared scientific and scholarly ideas with them, sang their songs, sometimes fell in love with them.

Another problem with the 'clash of civilizations' thesis is that it forces determinism into the study of the past. It takes as its starting point one of the world's currently most intractable political problems – the 'crisis' of the Middle East – and seeks to explain it by assuming an unchanging set of relationships between different religious cultures and their competing claims. Yet just as there was nothing inevitable about the origins of violent relations between Christians and Muslims in the eleventh century, neither was the subsequent course of holy war inevitable. One might argue, indeed, that so different were both Christian and Islamic societies in 1500 from what they had been in 1100, that it is remarkable that holy war still had a role to play at all.

Crusading as an activity and as an ideal evolved and changed constantly in the light of new thinking and in response to new situations. This makes it difficult to use the past as a mirror for the present. It does not, however, render knowledge of the past unnecessary. Understanding how and why the Crusades came about, why they took the course that they did, how they affected Europeans' dealings with people outside Christendom, and how they reflected changes in European society is vital if we are to understand the relationship between religious belief, political action and social forces that made Europe what it is today.

Further reading

Asbridge, Thomas. *The First Crusade: A New History* (London: Free Press, 2005).

——. *The Crusades: The War for the Holy Land* (London: Simon & Schuster, 2010).

Barber, Malcolm. *The Crusader States* (New Haven: Yale University Press, 2012).

Flori, Jean. *Richard the Lionheart: King and Knight,* trans. Jean Birrell (Edinburgh: Edinburgh University Press, 1999).

Frankopan, Peter. *The First Crusade: The Call from the East* (London: Bodley Head, 2012).

Hillenbrand, Carole. *The Crusades: Islamic Perspectives,* 2nd edition (Edinburgh: Edinburgh University Press, 2012).

Housley, Norman. *The Later Crusades 1274–1580: from Lyons to Alcazar* (Oxford: Oxford University Press, 1992).

——. *The Crusaders* (Stroud: Tempus, 2002).

——. *Fighting for the Cross: Crusading to the Holy Land* (New Haven: Yale University Press, 2008).

Jaspert, Nikolas. *The Crusades,* trans. Phyllis Jestice (London: Routledge, 2006).

Jotischky, Andrew. *Crusading and the Crusader States* (Harlow: Longman Pearson, 2004).

Kostick, Conor. *The Siege of Jerusalem: Crusade and Conquest in 1099* (London: Continuum, 2009).

Lyons, Malcolm, and D.E.P. Jackson. *Saladin: The Politics of the Holy War* (Cambridge: Cambridge University Press, 1982).

Madden, Thomas, and Donald Queller. *The Fourth Crusade: The Conquest of Constantinople,* 2nd edition (Philadelphia: University of Pennsylvania Press, 1997).

Mayer, Hans Eberhard. *The Crusades,* trans. John Gillingham, 2nd edition (Oxford: Oxford University Press, 1988).

Nicholson, Helen (ed.). *Palgrave Advances in the Crusades* (Basingstoke: Palgrave Macmillan, 2005).

Phillips, Jonathan. *The Second Crusade: Extending the Frontiers of Christendom* (New Haven: Yale University Press, 2007).

Phillips, Jonathan. *Holy Warriors. A Modern History of the Crusades* (London: Vintage, 2010).

Powell, James. *Anatomy of a Crusade, 1213–1221* (Philadelphia: University of Pennsylvania Press, 1986).

Richard, Jean. *Saint Louis: Crusader King of France*, trans. Jean Birrell, edited and abridged by Simon Lloyd (Cambridge: Cambridge University Press, 1992).

——. *The Crusades c.1071–c.1291*, trans. Jean Birrell (Cambridge: Cambridge University Press, 1999).

Riley-Smith, Jonathan. *The Crusades: A History*, 3rd edition (London: Bloomsbury, 2014).

——. *The First Crusaders 1095–1131* (Cambridge: Cambridge University Press, 1997).

Runciman, Steven. *A History of the Crusades*, 3 vols. (Cambridge: Cambridge University Press, 1951–4).

Tyerman, Christopher. *God's War: A New History of the Crusades* (London: Allen Lane, 2006).

——. *The Debate on the Crusades* (Manchester: Manchester University Press, 2011).

Index